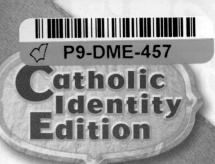

Catholic Identity Edition

Sadlier

We Believe

God Made the World

WITH PROJECT DISCIPLE

Pray
Learn
Celebrate
Share
Choose
Live

Kindergarten

Sadlier

This advanced publication copy has been printed prior to final publication and pending ecclesiastical approval.

Acknowledgments

Excerpts from the English translation of *The Roman Missal*, © 2010, International Committee on English in the Liturgy, Inc. All rights reserved.

Excerpts from the English translation of the *Catechism of the Catholic Church* for the United States of America, copyright © 1994, United States Catholic Conference, Inc.—Libreria Editrice Vaticana. English translation of the *Catechism of the Catholic Church: Modifications from the Editio Typica* copyright © 1997, United States Catholic Conference, Inc.—Libreria Editrice Vaticana. Used with permission.

Scripture excerpts are taken from the *New American Bible with Revised New Testament and Psalms* Copyright © 1991, 1986, 1970 Confraternity of Christian Doctrine, Inc., Washington, DC. Used with permission. All rights reserved. No part of the *New American Bible* may be reproduced by any means without permission in writing from the copyright owner.

Excerpts from the English translation of *A Book of Prayers* © 1982, ICEL; excerpts from the English translation of *The Liturgy of the Hours* © 1974, ICEL; excerpts from the English translation of *Book of Blessings* © 1988, ICEL.

English translation of the Lord's Prayer, the Nicene Creed, and Glory to the Father by the International Consultation on English Texts. (ICET)

Excerpt from *Evangelii Gaudium, Apostolic Exhortation on the Proclamation of the Gospel in Today's World*, Pope Francis, November 24, 2013, copyright © Vatican Publishing House, Libreria Editrice Vaticana.

Excerpt from *Sacrosanctum Concilium, Constitution on the Sacred Liturgy*, Pope Paul VI, December 4, 1963.

Excerpt from *Sacraments, Canon I*, Ecumenical Council of Trent, The Seventh Session, March 3, 1547.

Excerpt from *Gaudium et Spes, Pastoral Constitution of the Church in the Modern World*, Pope Paul VI, December 7, 1965.

Excerpts from *Catholic Household Blessings and Prayers (Revised Edition)* copyright © 2007, 1988 United States Catholic Conference, Inc. Washington, D.C. Used with permission. All rights reserved.

"We Believe, We Believe in God," © 1979, North American Liturgy Resources (NALR), 5536 NE Hassalo, Portland, OR 97213. All rights reserved. Used with permission. "Make A Joyful Noise," © 1995, Mark Friedman, Published by Oregon Catholic Press, 5536 NE Hassalo, Portland, OR 97213. All rights reserved. Used with permission. "I Know that God Loves Me," © 2000, Carey Landry. Published by OCP Publications, 5536 NE Hassalo, Portland, OR 97213. All rights reserved. Used with permission. "Advent Canon," © 2000, Carey Landry. Published by OCP Publications, 5536 NE Hassalo, Portland, OR 97213. All rights reserved. Used with permission. "Jesus Wants to Help Us," Music and text © 1999, Christopher Walker and Paule Freeburg, DC. Published by OCP Publications, 5536 NE Hassalo, Portland, OR 97213. All rights reserved. Used with permission. "Listen to Jesus," © 1999, Bernadette Farrell. Published by OCP Publications, 5536 NE Hassalo, Portland, OR 97213. All rights reserved. Used with permission. "I Am Your Friend," Music and text © 1999, Christopher Walker and Paule Freeburg, DC. Published by OCP Publications, 5536 NE Hassalo, Portland, OR 97213. All rights reserved. Used with permission. "Sing for Joy," © 1999, Bernadette Farrell. Published by OCP Publications, 5536 NE Hassalo, Portland, OR 97213. All rights reserved. Used with permission. "God Is a Part of My Life," © 1996, Carey Landry. Published by OCP Publications, 5536 NE Hassalo, Portland, OR 97213. All rights reserved. Used with permission. "Celebrate God," © 1973, 1998, Carey Landry, Carol Jean Kinghorn and North American Liturgy Resources (NALR). Published by OCP Publications, 5536 NE Hassalo, Portland, OR 97213. All rights reserved. Used with permission. "Sing a New Song," © 1972, 1974, Daniel L. Schutt. Administered by New Dawn Music, 5536 NE Hassalo, Portland, OR 97213. All rights reserved. Used with permission. "Shout from the Mountains," © 1992, Marie-Jo Thum. Published by OCP Publications, 5536 NE Hassalo, Portland, OR 97213. All rights reserved. Used with permission.

William H. Sadlier, Inc.
9 Pine Street
New York, NY 10005-4700

ISBN: 978-0-8215-3080-1

8 9 10 WEBC 22 21 20 19

Photo Credits

Cover: Corbis/DLILLC: *lion and lamb*; Dreamstime.com/Dzain: *wild goose chase*; Getty Images/Ron and Patty Thomas: *Maple Sugar trees landscape*; SuperStock/age fotostock/John Greim: *St. Bridget Church, Corwall, CT.* Interior: age fotostock/BEW Authors: R1 *bottom*; Craig Joiner: R6; Morales: R1 *center*; R. Wilken: R1 *top*. Alamy/Big Glass Eye: 132 *bottom*; Image Source: 38 *bottom left*; jump fotoagentur Susanne Treubel: R7 *top*; Susana Guzman: R31 *bottom*; LHB Photo: 268; Radius Images: 154 *center*; Wesley Roberts: R27; Steve Skjold: 269 *top right*; thislife pictures: R26 *top*; VStock: 103 *top*; Zoonar GmbII: R15. Art Resource, NY/Michael Escoffery: 135 *left*; Ricco-Maresca Gallery, NY, NY: 210. Jane Bernard: 61 *bottom right*, 15 *bottom*, 177 *top*, 187 *right*, 267 *top right*. Blend Images/Don Mason: R4 *center*. Bridgeman Images/Hamburger Kunsthalle, Hamburg, Germany: 271. Bruce Coleman Inc./Photoshot/Jane Burton: 15 *bottom left*, 57 *bottom left*. Karen Callaway: R31 *top*, 55, 56, 63 *bottom*, 188 *top*, 211. Comstock Images: 220 *top*. Corbis/Pablo Corral V: 38 *top left*; Digital Stock Corporation: 43 *background*; Reuters/Stefano Rellandini: R30; Michael St. Maur Sheil: 140 *top right*; Ariel Skelley: 67 *bottom right*, 176 *bottom*; Tom Stewart: 41 *top right*; Tetra Images: 133 *center right*, 177 *bottom*. Creatas: 104. The Crosiers/Gene Plaisted, OSC: R14, 18, 56 *top*, 64 *bottom*, 131, 141. Diaphor/Eureka StockLibrary: 63 *center*. Digital Vision/Gerry Ellis: 52 *center right*. Neal Farris: 11 *bottom right*, 13 *right*, 14 *left*, 23, 27, 45 *top*, 51, 53 *right*, 54, 61 *top left*, 81 *bottom right*, 81 *bottom center*, 82, 85, 88, 89, 90 *right*, 97 *right*, 103 *center bottom*, 103 *bottom*, 191 *left*, 193, 198, 217, 219 *top right*, 223, 242, 252 *right*, 267 *left*. Getty Images/AFP: 77 *top*; Jim Arbogast: 103 *center top*; James Baigrie: R9 *top*; Burke/Triolo Productions: 37 *bottom right*; China Tourism Press: 220 *bottom*; Jim Cummins: 25; De Agostini/G. Dagli Orti: 266; Phil Degginger: 176 *top*; Nicholas DeVore: 77 *bottom left*; Fuse: R26 *center*; Todd Gipstein: 227 *bottom*; Robert Glusic: 94 *top*; Sara Gray: 67 *left*; Charles Gupton: 244 *bottom left*; Peter Hince: 77 *bottom right*; Ed Honowitz: 7 *center*, 75 *center left*, 77 *center*; Sandra Ivany: 63 *top*; Gavriel Jecan: 52 *top left*; Sean Justice: 75 *center right*, 111 *bottom left*, 246 *top*; Bruce Laurance: G. Brad Lewis: 94 *top center*; Ken McGraw: 41 *left*; Laurence Monneret: 105; Marilyn Nieves: R9 *bottom right*; White Packert: 20 *top*; Daniel Pangbourne: 20 *bottom left*; Kevin Peterson: 81 *top left*; Photodisc: 10 *top*, 11 *top*, 13 *left*, 22, 24 *top right*, 35, 45 *center left*, 45 *center right*, 45 *bottom left*, 45 *bottom right*, 52 *left*, 233, 237 *right*, 238; Carol Polich Photo Workshops: R3 *bottom*; 89 *bottom left*; Andy Sacks: 17 *center left*, 24 *bottom right*, 38 *top right*; Marco Simoni: 184-185; Philip and Karen Smith: 24 *left*; Stockbyte: 38 *bottom right*, 45 *top left*, 223 *inset*; Charles Thatcher: 246 *bottom*; Camille Tokerud Photography Inc.: R26 *bottom*; Ross Whitaker: 220 *center*; Art Wolfe: 94 *center*; Yukmin: R9 *bottom left*. GoodSalt Inc./Linda Lovett: R19. Ken Karp: 10 *bottom*, 11 *bottom left*, 12, 14 *right*, 15 *bottom right*, 15 *center right*, 17 *center right*, 33, 43 *center*, 61 *top right*, 68, 69, 71, 79, 86, 87, 91, 93, 95, 97 *left*, 98, 101, 106, 109, 110, 113 *right*, 115, 117, 121 *left*, 121 *right*, 122 *right*, 123, 126, 132 *top left*, 133 *center left*, 135 *right*, 140 *bottom right*, 143, 147, 148, 151, 159, 162, 163, 164, 167, 168, 173, 175, 178, 179, 180, 181, 191 *center*, 192, 195, 197, 200 *center left*, 202, 207, 209, 215, 225, 231 *right*, 231 *left*, 233 *center*, 235, 244 *right*, 250, 256. Frans Lanting: 15 *top right*, 57 *top*. Greg Lord: 139 *bottom left*, 139 *right*, 191 *top*, 201, 213 *left*, 213 *right*, 191 *top*, 201, 213 *left*, 213 *right*, 214, 272. Masterfile/Premium Royalty-Free: R23. Cheryl & Leo Meyer: 94 *center bottom*. Lawrence Migdale: 20 *bottom right*. Myrleen Pearson: 154 *top*. Photodisc: 128. PhotoEdit/Robert Brenner: 111 *bottom right*; Jeff Greenberg: 111 *top*. Punchstock/Cultura: 41; Digital Vision: 52 *top right*. Used under permission from Shutterstock.com/Sushko Anastasia: R7 *bottom*; Inna Astakhova: 19 *bottom*, 243 *bottom*; Blinka: 52 *center right*; Natalia Bratslavsky: 53 *left*; Hluboki Dzianis: R9 *center*; edel: R14 *background*; Olesya Feketa: 67 *top right*; hoperan: 269 *top left*; Hasloo Group Production Studio: 263 *top*; iktash: R12; Tischenko Irina: 269 *bottom*; Tatiana Kasyanova: R21; Monkey Business Images: 76; Vira Mylyan-Monastryska: 270; Hana Stepanikova: 265 *bottom*; Vaclav Volrad: 263 *bottom*; matka_Wariatka: 94 *bottom*. SuperStock/Blend Images: R2, R3 *top*; Comstock/Exactostock: R4 *right*; Tetra Images: R4 *left*. Veer/UpperCut Images Photography: 132 *top right*. W.P. Wittman Ltd: 64 *top*, 139 *top left*, 187 *left*, 188 *right*, 237 *left*, 267 *bottom right*.

Illustrator Credits

Series Patterned Background: Evan Polenghi. Bernard Adnet: 49. Selina Alko: 97-98, 139-140, 142. Scott Angle: 74. Sheila Bailey: 229-230. Kristin Barr: 193, 209, 219, 251. Jared Beckstrand: 34, 116. Sarah Beise: R18, 30, 159. Linda Bronson: 143. Greta Buchart: 53-54. Chris Butler: 227. Antonio Cangemi: 35. Penny Carter: 96, 100. Emilie Chollat: 138. Lawrence Cleyet: 102, 108. Garry Colby: 57. Liz Conrad: 83. David Dean: 197-198, 250. David Diaz: 27, 202. Jane Dippold: 26, 44, 50, 163-164. Mena Dolobowsky: 174, 190, 232. Julie Downing: 171-172. Peter Fasolino: 221-222. Siri Weber-Feeney: 113-114. Dagmar Fehlau: 194, 200. Laura Freeman: 212, 216. Lisa Chauncy Guida: 121-122. Mike Gordon: 231. Myron Grossman: 151. Tim Haggerty: 92, 109. Franklin Hammond: 160, 166. April Hartman: 112. Steve Haskamp: 55-56. Steve Henry: 220. Joanna Hus: 19. Nathan Jarvis: 66, 182. Steve Johnson: 17, 31a-31b, 32, 250. W.B. Johnston: 265. Doreen Gay Kassel: 157. Michael Letzig: 153. Lori Lohstoeter: 47-48. Margaux Lucas: 80, 84. Diana Magnuson: R11, R13, 136-137, 142, 145, 150, 152, 155-156, 158, 161, 166, 167, 218, 226, 252. Bob Masheris: 169, 174. Bob McMahon: 213-214. Judith Moffatt: 99, 146, 150, 237-238. Keiko Motoyama: 93. Tate Nation: 223. Alan Neider: 149. John Nez: 6, 17, 46, 225. Miriam Nixon: 20, 25, 173. Michele Noiset: 217. Bob Ostrom: 42, Charlene Potts: 81, 82. Mike Radencich: 187-188. Olivia Rayner: 107. Victoria Raymond: 59, 60, 61, 62, 65, 66, 67, 68, 69, 70, 73, 74, 119, 120, 123, 124, 126, 127, 128, 131, 132, 175, 181, 182, 183, 186, 190, 233, 236, 239, 240. Tim Robinson: 135. Melissa Roger: 243. Zina Saunders: 105-106, 108, 142, 147-148, 201, 208, 247-248. Jack Savitsky: 216. Stacey Schuett: 129-130, 165. Clive Scruton: 241. David Sheldon: 245. Linda Solovic: 41. Ken Spengler: 101, 205-206, 251. Judy Stead: 144, 203, 208. Robert G. Steele: 196. Matt Straub: 85, 92, 252. Gerardo Suzan: 23-24. Susan Swan: 37, 42, 51, 52, 58. Marina Thompson: 204. Pam Thomson: 170. Elizabeth Trostli: 104. Jeremy Tugeau: 115, 116. Geraldo Valerio: 39-40, 228. Amy Vangsgard: 78. Tina Vey: 89, 90. Mark Weber: 210. Ann Wilson: 199. Jean Wisenbaugh: 36, 42, 102. Mike Wohnoutka: 71-72, 74. Amy Wummer: 16, 58, 224.

The Sadlier *We Believe* Program was drawn from the wisdom of the community. It was developed by nationally recognized experts in catechesis, curriculum, and child development. These teachers of the faith and practitioners helped us to frame every lesson to be age-appropriate and appealing. In addition, a team including respected catechetical, liturgical, pastoral, and theological experts shared their insights and inspired the development of the program.

Contributors to the inspiration and development are:

Dr. Gerard F. Baumbach
Professor Emeritus, Institute for Church Life
Director Emeritus of the Echo Program
University of Notre Dame

Carole M. Eipers, D.Min.
Vice President, Executive Director
 of Catechetics
William H. Sadlier, Inc.

Theological Consultants

His Eminence Donald Cardinal Wuerl, M.A., S.T.D.
Archbishop of Washington

Most Reverend Edward K. Braxton, Ph.D., S.T.D.
Official Theological Consultant
Bishop of Belleville

Reverend Joseph A. Komonchak, Ph.D.
Professor Emeritus of Theology and Religious Studies
The Catholic University of America

Most Reverend Richard J. Malone, Th.D.
Bishop of Buffalo

Reverend Monsignor John E. Pollard, S.T.L.
Pastor, Queen of All Saints Basilica
Chicago, IL

Scriptural Consultant

Reverend Donald Senior, CP, Ph.D., S.T.D.
Member, Pontifical Biblical Commission
President Emeritus of Catholic Theological Union
Chicago, IL

Catechetical and Liturgical Consultants

Patricia Andrews
Director of Religious Education
Our Lady of Lourdes Church,
Slidell, LA

Reverend Monsignor John F. Barry, P.A.
Pastor, American Martyrs Parish
Manhattan Beach, CA

Reverend Monsignor John M. Unger
Deputy Superintendent for Catechesis
 and Evangelization
Archdiocese of St. Louis

Thomas S. Quinlan
Director, Religious Education Office
Diocese of Joliet

Curriculum and Child Development Consultants

Brother Robert R. Bimonte, FSC
President, NCEA

Sr. Carol Cimino, SSJ, Ed.D.
Superintendent, Catholic Schools
Diocese of Buffalo

Gini Shimabukuro, Ed.D.
Professor Emeritus
Catholic Educational Leadership Program
School of Education
University of San Francisco

Catholic Social Teaching Consultants

John Carr
Director
Initiative on Catholic Social Thought and Public Life
Georgetown University

Joan Rosenhauer
Executive Vice President, U.S. Operations
Catholic Relief Services
Baltimore, MD

Inculturation Consultants

Allan Figueroa Deck, S.J., Ph.D., S.T.D.
Rector of Jesuit Community
Charles Casassa Chair of Catholic Social Values
Professor
Loyola Marymount University

Kirk P. Gaddy, Ed.D.
Middle School Team Leader/Religion Teacher
St. Francis International School
Silver Spring, MD

Reverend Nguyễn Việt Hưng
Vietnamese Catechetical Committee

Dulce M. Jiménez-Abreu
Director of Bilingual Programs
William H. Sadlier, Inc.

Mariology Consultant

Sister M. Jean Frisk, ISSM, S.T.L.
International Marian Research Institute
Dayton, OH

Media/Technology Consultants

Sister Judith Dieterle, SSL
Past President, National Association of
    Catechetical Media Professionals

Robert Methven
Vice President, Digital Publisher
William H. Sadlier, Inc.

Robert T. Carson
Media Design Director
William H. Sadlier, Inc.

Writing/Development Team

Rosemary K. Calicchio
Executive Vice President, Publisher

Blake Bergen
Director of Publications

Joanne McDonald
Editorial Director

Regina Kelly
Supervising Editor

William M. Ippolito
Director of Corporate Planning

Martin Smith
Planning and Analysis
    Project Director

Dignory Reina
Editor

Peggy O'Neill
Digital Content Manager

Contributing Writers
Christian Garcia
Kathy Hendricks
Shannon Jones
Theresa MacDonald
Gloria Shahin

Suzan Laroquette
Director of Catechetical
    Consultant Services

Judith A. Devine
National Sales Consultant

Victor Valenzuela
National Religion Consultant

Publishing Operations Team

Carole Uettwiller
Vice President of Planning and
    Technology

Vince Gallo
Senior Creative Director

Francesca O'Malley
Art/Design Director

Cheryl Golding
Production Director

Monica Reece
Senior Production Manager

Jovito Pagkalinawan
Electronic Prepress Director

Design/Image Staff
Kevin Butler, Nancy Figueiredo,
Stephen Flanagan, Lorraine Forte,
Debrah Kaiser, Cesar Llacuna,
Bob Schatz, Karen Tully

Production Staff
Monica Bernier, Robin D'Amato,
Rachel Jacobs, Carol Lin,
Vincent McDonough,
Yolanda Miley, Laura Rotondi,
Allison Stearns

We are grateful to our loyal *We Believe* users whose insights and suggestions have inspired *We Believe: Catholic Identity Edition*—the premier faith formation tool built on the six tasks of catechesis.

Contents

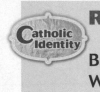

UNIT 3 Jesus Shows Us God's Love 133

SEASONAL CHAPTERS

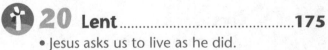

UNIT 4 Jesus Wants Us to Share God's Love.........................191

We Believe

The *We Believe* program will help us to

learn   celebrate

share

and

live our Catholic faith.

Throughout the year we will hear about many saints and holy people.

Saint Frances of Rome   Saint Martin de Porres

Saint Francis of Assisi   Mary, Mother of God's Son

Saint Gianna Beretta Molla   Saint Patrick

Saint John Bosco   Saint Peter

Saint Joseph   Saint Rose of Lima

Saint Kateri Tekakwitha   Saint Thérèse of Lisieux

Saint Katharine Drexel

Together, let us grow as a community of faith.

Welcome!

is an open Bible. When we see it with a blue Scripture reference, what follows is a paraphrase of the Bible.

When we see a black reference like this (John 13:34) that passage is directly from the Bible.

WE GATHER

When we see WE GATHER we come together as a class.

Then we

think about

talk about

at school

Life

in our church

at home

in our neighborhood

WE BELIEVE

Each day we learn more about God.

When we see WE BELIEVE we listen carefully.

We learn about the ways God loves us.

We also learn about the ways we can love God.

WE BELIEVE

Each day we share with one another.

We might
- draw
- act out
- circle
- imagine.

There are all kinds of activities!

🏃 Draw yourself here.

When we see 🏃 we do an activity.

This year you are in the *We Believe* Kindergarten class. We are so happy you are with us!

WE RESPOND

When we see WE RESPOND we share ways that we can love God and one another.

We can respond by

- drawing something
- talking about our thoughts and feelings
- singing and praying.

How can you thank God for loving you?

When we see **We Believe** we know it's time to read our We Believe Book.

Let's Celebrate

Our *We Believe* Kindergarten Class

When we see the **Let's Celebrate** page we know we will pray and sing.

✝ **We Pray**

People who love us make love grow.
Thank you, God, for our family.

Let us sing the *We Believe* song!

🎵 **We Believe, We Believe in God**

We believe in God;
We believe, we believe in Jesus;
We believe in the Spirit who gives us life.
We believe, we believe in God.

You are on a journey to continue to grow as a disciple of Jesus Christ. You can strengthen your Catholic Identity through these new features:

Catholic Identity Retreats

Bringing the Retreat Home

Why We Believe As a Catholic Family

Catholic Identity Q & A

Catholic Identity Home Companion

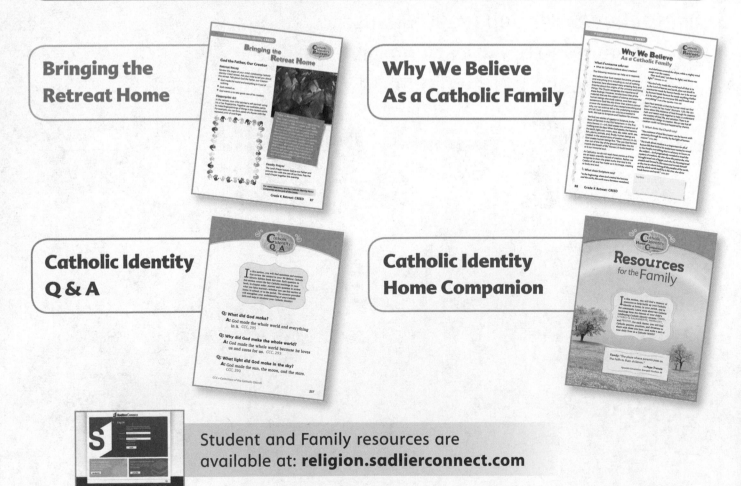

Student and Family resources are available at: **religion.sadlierconnect.com**

God the Father, Our Creator

Part 1   I Open My Heart

God made our world. God made everything. Creation is God's gift!

Think of something from God's creation that you see in each season. Draw those things in the boxes below.

Summer	Fall
Winter	Spring

God the Father, Our Creator

Part 2   We Come Together for Prayer

Leader: Thank you, God, for creating us! We are all God's children. Repeat after me: God, "I praise you, so wonderfully you made me" (Psalm 139:14).

All: God, "I praise you, so wonderfully you made me" (Psalm 139:14).

🎵 **God Made People**

   (*"Here We Go 'Round the Mulberry Bush"*)

God made people out of love,
out of love, out of love.
God made people out of love.
Let's join our hands and
    thank him.

God wants us to share his love,
share his love, share his love.
God wants us to share
    his love.
Let's all shake hands and
    thank him.

Amen.

God the Father, Our Creator

Part 3 I Cherish God's Word

"God looked at everything he had made, and he found it very good." (Genesis 1:31)

LISTEN to the reading from Scripture. Pay close attention to the reading.

REFLECT on what you heard. Think about:

- All of God's creation is very good. That includes you! What does God see that is very good in you?

SHARE your thoughts and feelings with God in prayer. Speak to God as a friend.

CONTEMPLATE or sit quietly and think about God's Word in the Scripture passage from the Book of Genesis above.

God the Father, Our Creator

Part 4 I Value My Catholic Faith

God wants us to take good care of creation.
We can help take care of the earth.
We can care for everything God created.

Join *God's Creation Crew*!
Draw a picture of caring
for God's creation on
the badge. Wear your
badge proudly!

God's Creation Crew

God the Father, Our Creator

Part 5   I Celebrate Catholic Identity

You are God's child. You are special. God even made your fingertips special! No other person has the same fingerprints you do.

Use your fingerprint to create a picture of God's superstar—you!

I AM WONDERFULLY
MADE . . .

BY GOD, MY FATHER
AND CREATOR!

God the Father, Our Creator

Part 6   I Honor My Catholic Identity

Leader: God, our Father and Creator, you created us out of love. Help us to love you and all of your creation. Echo this prayer.

Leader: Blessed are you, my God!
All: Blessed are you, my God!

Leader: You fill my heart with love.
All: You fill my heart with love.

Leader: So good are you, my God!
All: So good are you, my God!

Leader: Creation is your gift from above.
All: Creation is your gift from above. Amen.

(Poem inspired by the hymn "O God of Loveliness" by Saint Alphonsus Liguori)

Catholic Identity Retreat

Bringing the Retreat Home

God the Father, Our Creator

Retreat Recap

Review the pages of your child's *Celebrating Catholic Identity: Creed* retreat. Ask your child to tell you about the retreat. Talk about God the Father, our Creator:

- God made the world and everything in it out of nothing.
- God created us.
- God wants us to take good care of his creation.

Fingerprint Art

In the retreat, your child painted a self-portrait using his or her fingerprints. Together use washable paints to make fingerpaintings of things in the created world. For example, you can form petals of a flower with the repeated print of one finger.

Take a Moment

Your child's retreat focused on appreciating God's creation. Take a "nature walk" with your child in a place where you can readily observe the gifts of God's creation, such as flowers, trees, or other plants; birds and other creatures; a pond, a stream, or another body of water; and shells, pebbles, or rocks. Invite your child to think of yourselves as "explorers," discussing what you see and what is special about it. You may wish to photograph what you see or take away a small natural memento of your excursion, such as a colorful leaf.

Family Prayer

The Lord's Prayer honors God as our Father and entrusts him with the care of our lives. Pray the Lord's Prayer together this evening.

For more resources, see the *Catholic Identity Home Companion* at the end of this book.

Why We Believe
As a Catholic Family

What if someone asks us:

- What do Catholics believe about creation?

The following resources can help us to respond:

We believe that God created the entire universe and everything in it, including us, out of nothing. Scientists have discovered many amazing facts and theories about the origins of the universe and living things. The Church recognizes the importance of these findings. However, we also know that all the materials that are the subject of science, and even the human beings who study science, owe their very existence to God! We also know that science cannot answer the questions of who created everything and why, nor can science tell us the underlying purpose of it all. Such questions can only be answered in faith. We look to Scripture and Tradition for answers.

We find two stories of creation in Scripture, in the Book of Genesis in the Old Testament. In the first story (Genesis 1:1—2:4), God creates the universe out of nothing over six days. When God speaks, the heavens, the earth, light, sun, moon, stars, sky, water, earth, sea, fish, plants, animals, and, finally, human beings are created. In the second story of creation (Genesis 2:5–25), God creates human beings first. "The LORD God formed man out of the clay of the ground and blew into his nostrils the breath of life." (Genesis 2:7) Human persons are created in the image of God and are both body and soul.

As Catholics, we do not read these stories as if they are an exact scientific record of creation. Rather, we recognize in them the great truths that God is the Creator of all and has made us in his image, creating us body and soul.

🌿 What does Scripture say?

"In the beginning, when God created the heavens and the earth, the earth was a formless wasteland, and darkness covered the abyss, while a mighty wind swept over the waters.

Then God said, 'Let there be light,' and there was light.'" (Genesis 1:1–3)

"The God who made the world and all that is in it, the Lord of heaven and earth, does not dwell in sanctuaries made by human hands, nor is he served by human hands because he needs anything. Rather it is he who gives to everyone life and breath and everything." (Acts of the Apostles 17:24–25)

Saint Paul reminds us that the human mind can find God "in what he has made" (Romans 1:20). We can know about the existence of God through his creation. Faith and reason work together to help us understand the mystery of God, life, and salvation. There is an extraordinary design to creation. We can see that all creation could not have just happened by chance.

🌿 What does the Church say?

"The existence of God the Creator can be known with certainty through his works, by the light of human reason." (CCC, 286)

"God progressively revealed to Israel the mystery of creation. He who chose the patriarchs, who brought Israel out of Egypt, and who by choosing Israel created and formed it, this same God reveals himself as the One to whom belong all the peoples of the earth, and the whole earth itself." (CCC, 287)

Notes:

God Gives Us Many Gifts

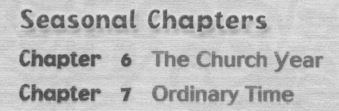

Seasonal Chapters

DEAR FAMILY

In Unit 1 your child will grow as a disciple of Jesus by:

- recognizing the gifts God gives us in creation
- giving thanks and praise to God for all his gifts
- understanding that God shows his love for us through creation
- learning that everything God made is good
- caring for God's gifts of water, land, and animals.

Saint Stories

In this unit, your child will learn that God created all the animals. Share the story of Saint Francis of Assisi who was known for his love of all God's creatures. Learn more about him at *Lives of the Saints* at **www.webelieveweb.com**.

More to Explore

There is an estimate that there are more than 3 million kinds of animals on the earth. See how many different kinds of animals you and your child can name. Then visit the zoo to learn about unfamiliar animals. Thank God for all animals!

Reality Check

"Parents have the first responsibility for the education of their children."

(Catechism of the Catholic Church, 2223)

Picture This

Together, look at the images on pages 28–29 in your child's text. Have your child share what he or she likes to do when the sun is shining and when the moon and stars are out. Share the things you like to do at these times. Then do one of the activities together!

Make it Happen

Your child will learn about God's gifts. Talk about your favorite gifts. Decide on ways you can take care of these gifts.

Take Home

Each chapter in your child's *We Believe* Kindergarten text offers a "Take Home" activity that invites your family to support your child's journey to more fully become a disciple of Christ.

Be ready for this unit's Take Home:

Chapter 1: Thanking God for his special gifts

Chapter 2: Praying with candlelight

Chapter 3: Conserving water

Chapter 4: Reducing, reusing, and recycling at home

Chapter 5: Learning about caring for animals

God Made All Things

WE GATHER

📖 Psalm 89:12

God, you made the whole world and everything in it.

What can you tell your friends about our wonderful world?

WE BELIEVE

God made the whole world.

God loves us.
God cares for us.
God filled our world
with many things.

 Look at the pictures.
What do you see?

Everything God made is good.

All things are gifts from God.

God gave us the ☁.

God gave us the 🏖.

God gave us the 〰.

🧍 Show where you can find these gifts from God. Add other gifts God made.

WE RESPOND

What is wonderful about God's world?

Draw yourself in God's wonderful world.

Praise for God

Thank God for all he has made.

Thank him for the sun and the moon.

Thank him for the shining stars.

Thank God for all the people.
Praise God for all he has made.

Fold

Thank God for the mountains and hills.
Thank him for the deep oceans.

Thank God for fish and for birds.
Thank him for animals, wild and tame.

Fold

Let's Celebrate
God's Gifts

✝ **We Pray**

God, we praise you.
God, we thank you.

Pray
Learn
Celebrate
Share
Choose
Live

Fill the scene with God's gifts.

Share your picture with a friend.

Take Home

Talk together about the special gifts God has given to your family. Pray a family prayer of thanksgiving.

God Gives Us Light

WE GATHER

Genesis 1:3

God said, "Let there be light."

What makes our world warm and bright?

WE BELIEVE

God made the sun.

God loves us.
God cares for us.
God gave us the sun to help us.

Draw something you like to do when the ☀ is shining.

God made the moon and the stars.

God gave us the moon and the stars.
They brighten our nights.

Draw something you like to do when the 🌑 and ⭐ light the sky.

WE RESPOND

Where can you see God's gift of light?

🎵 What a Gift!
("This Old Man")

We see the sun.
We see the moon.
We see the light
Both day and night.
Thank you, God, for giving us the light.
Thank you, God, for your gift of light.

A Great Gift

Thank you, God, for the gift of light.
Thank you for the morning.

Thank you for the night.
Thank you, God, for your
great gift of light!

Fold

Thank you for
the afternoon.

Fold

Thank you for
the evening.

Let's Celebrate
God's Gift of Light

✝ **We Pray**

📖 Genesis 1:3–5

Read to Me

God said, "Let there be light," and there was light. God saw how good the light was. God then separated the light from the darkness. God called the light "day," and the darkness he called "night." Thus evening came, and morning followed—the first day.

Thank you, God, for giving us the light.
Thank you, God, for your gift of light.

Pray Learn Celebrate Share Choose Live

Draw a ✔ next to the things that give us light.

Thank God for the gift of light.

Take Home

After the sun has set, gather your family around a special light source (a lamp, a candle, etc.). Hold hands and thank God for bringing light to the darkness.

God Gives Us Water

WE GATHER

📖 Genesis 1:10

God made the land and the waters.

How does water feel?
How does water sound?

God made water.

God's gift of water is everywhere.

👤 Trace the path of the falling raindrops.

God gives us water to live.

God loves us.
God cares for us.
He gives us water to help us.
God's gift of water can be
used in many ways.

How is this family using water?
Circle the ways.

WE RESPOND

God wants us to use his gifts with care.

👤 Color the 💧 by the pictures that show how we take care of water.

What Gift of God Am I?

I belong in this dish for the fish.

What wonderful gift of God am I? Add me in the picture.

- - - - - - - - - - - Fold - - - - - - - - - - -

I am a gift from God.
I am

WATER

I cool your feet in the heat.
What wonderful gift of God am I?
Add me in the picture.

First, I fall to the ground.
Then things grow all around.
What wonderful gift of God am I?
Add me in the picture.

Fold

Let's Celebrate
God's Gift of Water

✝ **We Pray**

For water here,
For water there,
For water, water everywhere,
We thank you, God.

PROJECT DISCIPLE

Pray
Learn
Celebrate
Share
Choose
Live

Draw a ✔ under the picture that shows the child taking care of God's gift of water.

How can you care for God's gift of water?

Take Home

Together brainstorm ways your family can conserve water. Then put these ideas into action!

God Gives Us the Land

WE GATHER

📖 Genesis 1:10

God called the land "earth."

What kind of things fill the land?

God filled the land with many gifts.

God loves us.
God cares for us.
He gave us things that grow from the earth.

Color the things that grow from the earth.
Show how you enjoy these gifts from God.

God wants us to take care of the gifts of the land.

God does not want us to waste his gifts.
How can we care for God's gifts?

Match each square with a way you can care.

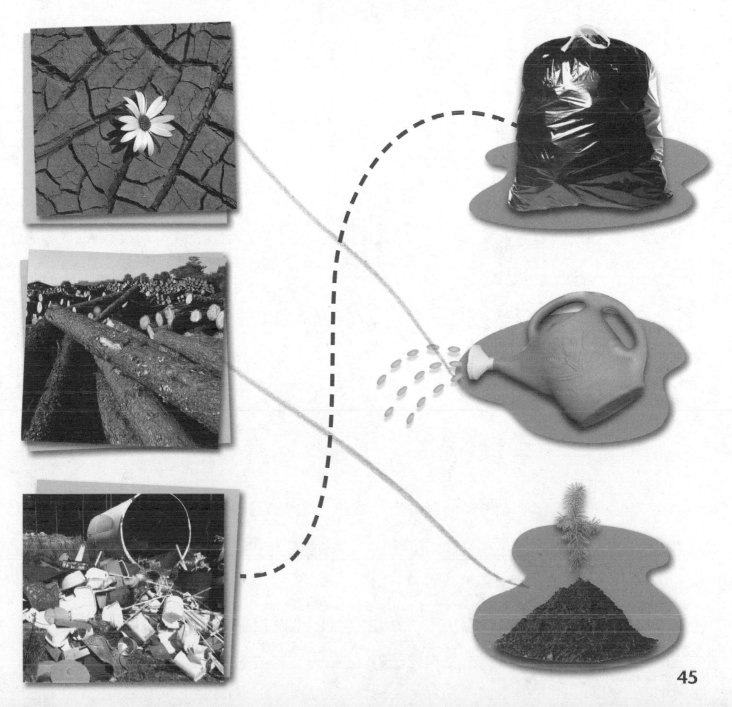

WE RESPOND

How can we share God's gifts?

Talk about each picture.

Saint Rose of Lima

Long ago, in Lima, Peru, there lived a young girl named Isabelle.

People said she was as pretty as a rose. So her family began to call her Rose.

Fold

Many poor people came to Rose's home for help. She took care of the poor and sick. She spent every day sharing God's love.

2

Rose wanted to help her own poor family. She planted a flower garden. She sold the flowers she grew.

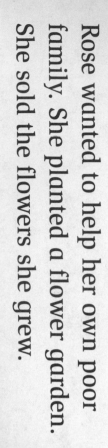

Fold

Rose loved God very much.
Rose loved all people.

Let's Celebrate
God's Gift of Land

✝ We Pray

For ⛰️, we thank you, God.

For 🌵, we thank you, God.

For 🪨, we thank you, God.

For ⛰️, we thank you, God.

For the land and all that fills it,
we thank you, God.

The world is made of land and water.

Color the spaces with L  green .

Color the spaces with W blue .

L

W

W

L

Add stars, the sun, and the moon.

Take Home

Try to put the words *reduce*, *reuse*, and *recycle* into action in your home by making less trash, creatively reusing items that would otherwise be thrown away, and recycling those items that must be.

God Made the Animals

WE GATHER

📖 Genesis 1:25

God made all kinds of animals. "God saw how good it was."

What is your favorite animal?

51

God made all kinds of animals.

God loves us.
God cares for us.
God filled the world with animals.

Pretend you are your favorite animal.
Let your friends guess what you are.

Draw your favorite animal.
Could you take care of this animal?
How?

WE BELIEVE

Animals are gifts from God.

How many animals can you name?
Did God make them all look the same?

Give the lamb a wooly coat.

Add brown spots to the giraffe.

Give the lion a mane.

53

WE RESPOND

How can you thank God for animals? Taking care of them is one way to thank him.

Circle ways to take care of animals.

A Special Blessing

Next week is the Feast of Saint Francis. He shared God's love with everyone.

This is what Saint Francis did. He blessed all the animals.

Let's Celebrate

God's Gift of Animals

✝ **We Pray**

🎵 **God Made All the Animals**

("Here We Go 'Round the Mulberry Bush")

God made all the animals,
The animals, the animals.
God made all the animals
God made our animal friends.

Have you seen an elephant walk?
An elephant walk, an elephant walk?
Have you seen an elephant walk?
God made this animal friend.

Have you heard a lion roar?
A lion roar, a lion roar?
Have you heard a lion roar?
God made this animal friend.

PROJECT DISCIPLE

Read the story.

 has a  .

 walks the  with a  .

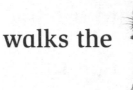 throws a  to the .

 washes the 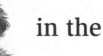 in the  .

 gives the  food and water .

How would you care for a pet?

Take Home

Find children's books at the library or bookstore that help your family to learn about caring for animals.

The Church Year

WE GATHER

Psalm 98:4

"Shout with joy to the LORD,
all the earth;
break into song; sing praise."

What do you like to do when you celebrate?

God wants us to celebrate his love for us.

We celebrate God's love in many ways.
We pray to him with our families.
We sing to him with our friends.

Draw yourself celebrating.

We celebrate the Church year.

We celebrate God's love all year.
We have special times of celebration.
These times help us to remember
God's love.

🤸 Act out some ways we
celebrate God's love.

♫ Make a Joyful Noise

Chorus
Make a joyful noise to our God on high!
  Make a joyful noise to our God!

Praise God with the trumpet blast,
  praise God with the cymbal crash.
Praise God with a joyful dance,
  praise the name of our God! (Chorus)
Praise God with the strings and reed,
  praise God with your melodies.
Praise God with a symphony,
  praise the name of our God! (Chorus)

We Celebrate All Year

We use
God's gifts when
we celebrate.

Fold

God's gifts help us
to remember his love.
They help us to celebrate
all year long.

We use water
and light.

Fold

We use flowers
and plants, too.

Let's Celebrate
All Year

✝ **We Pray**

Leader: We celebrate when it's sunny.

All: Praise God!

Leader: We celebrate when it's snowy.

All: Praise God!

Leader: We celebrate when the flowers bloom.

All: Praise God!

Leader: We celebrate when the leaves are falling.

All: Praise God!

Leader: We celebrate all year long!

All: Praise God!

PROJECT DISCIPLE

 Draw a ✔ next to the ways to celebrate God's love.

Take Home

Your family can celebrate God's love together. Find some ways to do this each day!

Ordinary Time

WE GATHER

📖 Mark 12:30

Love God with all your heart, with all your mind, and with all your strength. Love your neighbor as yourself.

What person do you know who takes special care of everyone?

All during the year we celebrate Jesus' love.

Jesus had many friends.
They celebrated his love.
They tried to be like him.

Jesus' friends lived
their lives loving God.
They are
called saints.

Saint Peter was one of
Jesus' first friends.
He told many people
about Jesus.

Saint Patrick was a
bishop in Ireland.
He taught the people
there about God.

We celebrate Ordinary Time.

Saints always tried to share God's love with others.

Saint Martin de Porres lived in Peru. He took care of people who were poor and hungry.

Saint Katharine Drexel lived in the United States. She taught children about Jesus.

WE RESPOND

We are called to be saints, too.
We do this by loving God and loving others.
What can you do to show love for God?
What can you do to show love for others?

Draw yourself here and write your name under your picture.

Reagan

Saint Joseph

Joseph was a good man. He lived in Nazareth with Mary and Jesus.

1

Fold

Joseph is a saint.

Saint Joseph

4

Joseph loved God very much. Joseph cared for Mary and Jesus.

Fold

Joseph showed God his love by the things he said and did.

Let's Celebrate
The Saints

✝ **We Pray**

🎵 **When the Saints Go Marching In**

Oh, when the saints go marching in,
Oh, when the saints go marching in,
O Lord, I want to be in that number,
When the saints go marching in.

Tell what is happening in each picture.

Color the ♡ under the picture that shows
the children showing love for others.

Take Home

Find out if anyone in your family is named for a saint.
If so, learn about the saint together.

God Is Our Creator

Seasonal Chapters

DEAR FAMILY

Pray
Learn
Celebrate
Share
Choose
Live

In Unit 2 your child will grow as a disciple of Jesus by:

- learning that God our Creator made and loves all people
- using the senses God gave us to discover God's world
- seeing the ways we can learn about God in our families
- sharing God's love by caring for our families and friends
- celebrating all of God's gifts in prayer.

Question Corner

Each of us experiences the world through God's gift of our senses. Together, ask your family members and friends which of the senses is most important to them and why. Talk with your child about people who cannot see or cannot hear and ways we can show respect for them.

Make it Happen

We all learn about God with our families and friends. Talk with your child about the people who have helped you to learn about God and what they taught you. Ask your child to share one thing they have learned about God with a family member or friend.

Show That You Care

Together discuss family members, friends, or neighbors who are having difficulties—for example illness or job loss—and who may need a reminder of God's love. Make a *God loves you!* sign for one or some of those people. Send it by mail or, if possible, deliver it together.

Pray Today

Together make a list of all the people who are important to your family. Have your child decorate the list and display it where you say nighttime prayers. Ask God to bless all the people on your list.

Reality Check

"Parents must regard their children as *children of God* and respect them as *human persons*."

(*Catechism of the Catholic Church*, 2222)

Take Home

Each chapter in your child's *We Believe* Kindergarten text offers a "Take Home" activity that invites your family to support your child's journey to more fully become a disciple of Christ.

Be ready for this unit's Take Home:

Chapter 8: Learning about your family's heritage

Chapter 9: Celebrating family members' unique traits

Chapter 10: Planning a family dinner that celebrates the senses

Chapter 11: Sharing God's love as a family

Chapter 12: Thanking God for family friends

God Made All People

WE GATHER

📖 Acts of the Apostles 17:25

God "gives to everyone life and breath and everything."

What would you like to ask the people in these pictures?

God made everyone.

God made all people good.
God gave people many gifts.
He gave people the world and
all the good things in it.

Add people to this picture.
Show them enjoying God's world.

WE BELIEVE

God loves all people.

There are people in every
part of the world.
God loves all of them.
He wants them to love him.
God wants all people
to share his love.

✗ Add yourself in the picture.

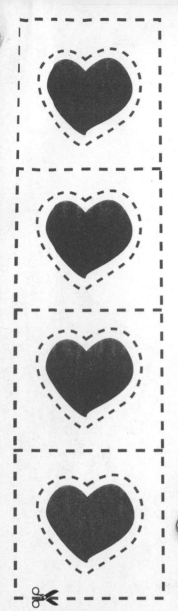

WE RESPOND

Cut out the hearts at the side of the page. Look at each picture. Talk about the way people are sharing God's love. If this is a way you can share love, put a heart near the picture.

The People We See

Here are people wearing different kinds of clothes.

Who made these people?

God made all people.

Fold

Here are people eating different kinds of foods.

Who made these people?

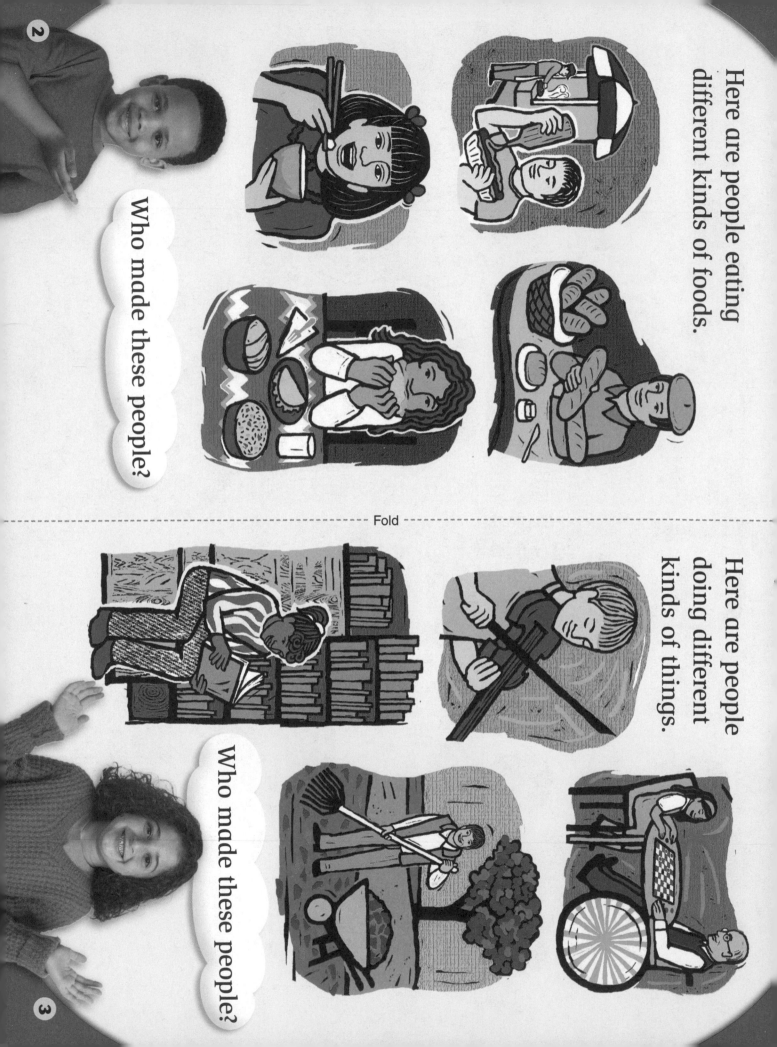

Here are people doing different kinds of things.

Who made these people?

Let's Celebrate
God's Gift of People

✝ **We Pray**

🎵 **God Made People**

("Here We Go 'Round the Mulberry Bush")

God made people out of love,
out of love, out of love.
God made people out of love.
Let's join our hands and thank him.

God wants us to share his love,
share his love, share his love.
God wants us to share his love.
Let's all shake hands and thank him.

PROJECT DISCIPLE

Finish the prayer with pictures.

God, you made

Thank you for loving

I want to share your love with

Amen.

Take Home

Share family stories, interview relatives, and spark curiosity about your family's heritage.

God Made Us

WE GATHER

📖 Psalm 139:14

God, "I praise you, so wonderfully you made me."

Imagine you are meeting someone for the first time. Tell this person about yourself.

God made you.

God made you special.
There is no other person exactly like you.

Here I am.

My name is

_____

_____

God loves you.

God loves you just the way you are.
God never stops loving you.

GOD LOVES ME!

Color this important message.
Remember it always.

We thank God for his love.
We can tell God we love him.

 In sign language,

is the sign for **I love you.**

Make this sign with your hand.
Raise it above your head to say,
"I love you, God."

You Can Tell God Anything

You can talk to God anytime.
You can tell God anything.

God, this is my favorite color.

God, this is a picture of my favorite story.

God, this is my favorite food.

Fold

God, this is my favorite
toy or game.

Let's Celebrate
God's Gift of Me

✝ **We Pray**

🎵 **I Know That God Loves Me**
From the top of my head,
from the top of my head,
To the ends of my toes,
to the ends of my toes,
I know that God loves me.
(Repeat)

I know, I know, I know, I know,
I know that God loves me.

From my fingertips,
from my fingertips,
To the smile on my lips,
to the smile on my lips,
I know that God loves me.
(Repeat)

I know, I know, I know, I know,
I know that God loves me.

91

PROJECT DISCIPLE

Tell about yourself by circling your choices.

Which is your favorite color?

blue green red

orange yellow purple

Which is your favorite activity?

Which is your favorite season?

Share your choices with a friend.

Take Home

Family members may share certain traits and characteristics but each person is unique. Celebrate this by pointing out unique traits in each other in positive ways.

God Helps Us to Discover

10

WE GATHER

Psalm 63:5

God, "I will lift up my hands, calling on your name."

What are these children discovering about God's world?

God gives us our senses.

God gives us the gift of our senses.

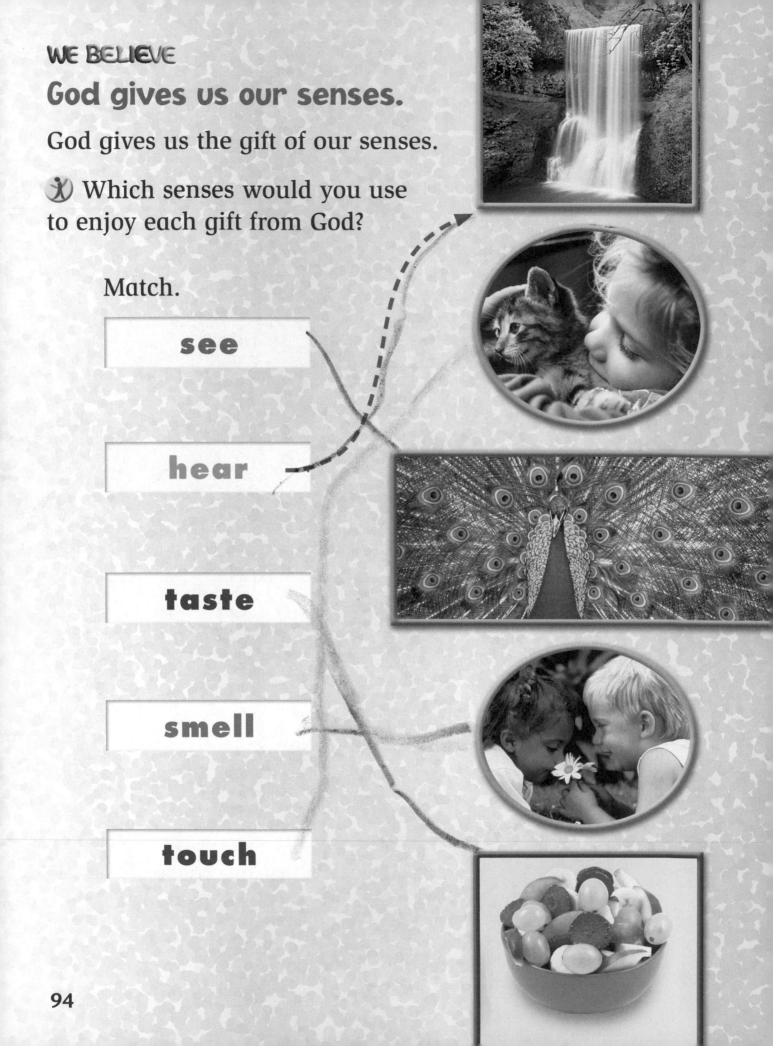 Which senses would you use to enjoy each gift from God?

Match.

see

hear

taste

smell

touch

We use our senses to discover God's world.

Go on a discovery walk.
Find out more about God's world.

 Draw things you see, hear,
touch, taste, and smell.

♫ God Gave Me My Senses

("Mary Had a Little Lamb")

God gave me my 👂👂 to hear,

ears to hear, ears to hear.

God gave me my 👂👂 to hear,

and this is what I hear. (Tell what you hear.)

Add these verses.

- God gave me my 👄 to taste.
- God gave me my 👁 👁 to see.
- God gave me my 👃 to smell.

God's Gifts—
My Senses

I use my senses to enjoy God's world.

Fold

I use my senses to show my love for God.

4

2

I use my senses to learn.

Fold

3

I use my senses to show love for myself and others.

Let's Celebrate
Our Senses

✝ **We Pray**

God, help me to use my senses to discover more about your world.

Leader: God, bless my eyes.

All: They help me to discover more about your world.

- God, bless my ears. (All)
- God, bless my nose. (All)
- God, bless my mouth. (All)
- God, bless my hands. (All)

Pray
Learn
Celebrate
Share
Choose
Live

Draw something you like to

see

touch

smell

taste

hear

Take Home

Plan a family dinner that celebrates all the senses. Include your child in the planning. Decorate, cook, enjoy music, talk, and celebrate together.

We Learn About God with Our Families

11

WE GATHER

📖 Psalm 136:1

Praise God, who is so good,
God's love lasts forever.

Where do you think this family is going?
Where do you like to go with your family?

Our families help us to discover God's world.

God wants families to spend time together.

Talk about each picture. What is the family discovering about God's world?

 Circle the pictures that show things you like to do with your family.

What else do families like to do together?

WE BELIEVE

Our families share God's love.

Our families show us God's love.

Match.

Families keep us safe.

Families teach us to share.

Families care for others.

Families talk things over with us.

WE RESPOND

We do things with our family
to share God's love.
We do things for our family
to share God's love.

Show how your family can
share God's love.

Draw a picture of your family.

Share your picture with your family.

God Cares for Our Families

📖 Psalm 23

The Lord is our shepherd.
He takes care of us.

Fold

God's love will always be with us.

2

God shows us the way to be good.

3

God watches over us. He helps us to be safe.

Fold

Let's Celebrate

God's Gift of Our Families

✝ **We Pray**

All: God, help us share your love.

Leader:
- With our family, (All)

- With our mothers, fathers, brothers, and sisters, (All)

- With our grandparents, aunts, uncles, and cousins, (All)

- With our godparents and friends, (All)

- With all people, (All)

PROJECT DISCIPLE

Listen to the story. Color the picture.

Read to Me
Saint Gianna shared God's love with others.

Saint Gianna was a daughter and sister.
She shared God's love with her family.

Saint Gianna was a mother.
She shared God's love with her children.

Saint Gianna was a doctor.
She shared God's love with her patients.

www.webelieveweb.com

Take Home
Whenever your family shows it cares, or shares with others, remember and remind each other that you are sharing God's love.

We Learn About God with Our Friends

12

WE GATHER

"Let everything that has breath give praise to the LORD!"

(Psalm 150:6)

Why do you like to be with your friends?

WE BELIEVE

Friends are special gifts from God.

Together we can discover God's world.
We can talk with each other.
We can listen and learn.
We can help each other.

🧍 Draw a picture of
your special friends.

We show our friends God's love.

Friends can show God's love every day.

Which picture shows friends sharing with each other? Draw a ▢ by it.

Which picture shows friends helping each other? Draw a △ by it.

Which picture shows friends helping other people? Draw a ● by it.

WE RESPOND

Friends can share God's love.
Friends can help each other.

Find the path to the Good
Friends' Garden. Talk about the
pictures that are on that path.

Good Friends' Garden

POPCORN

START

MUD

FRIENDS WITH GOD

Saints are friends of God.
Saints are our friends, too.
Saints help us to learn about God.
I can name some saints. Can you?

BOOK OF SAINTS

------------------------------ Fold ------------------------------

Saint Thérèse of Lisieux was a friend of God. She helped people all over the world. She prayed for them.

Saint Frances of Rome
was a friend of God.
She helped hungry people.
She gave them food.

Fold

Saint Martin de Porres
was a friend of God.
He helped sick people.
He cared for them.

Let's Celebrate

Friends

✝ **We Pray**

🎵 **The Gifts of God's Love**
("Did You Ever See a Lassie?")

Let's celebrate together,
together, together.
Let's celebrate together
God's great love for us.

God gives us our families.
He gives us our good friends.
Let's celebrate together
The gifts of God's love.

PROJECT DISCIPLE

Tell what is happening in each picture.

Color the ♡ over the picture of the children showing God's love.

Take Home

Think about your family's friends and the times you share. Thank God for these special people and times.

Advent

WE GATHER

Come, Lord Jesus!

How do you wait for someone special?

God gives us the greatest gift.

God sent his Son to the world.
God's Son would share his love with everyone.

God's Son would be the Light of the World.
To help you remember, finish this sun.
Cut out small pieces of yellow and
orange paper.
Put paste on the empty spaces.
Then put the colored paper on these spaces.

We celebrate Advent.

God chose Mary to be the Mother
of his Son.
Mary and her husband, Joseph,
waited for the Son of God to be born.
They would name him Jesus.

Trace over the dots.
Show how Mary and Joseph are
getting ready for Jesus.

WE RESPOND

We get ready to celebrate the coming of the Son of God.
We get ready by sharing and caring.

Draw a picture in each box.
Show how you will share and care.

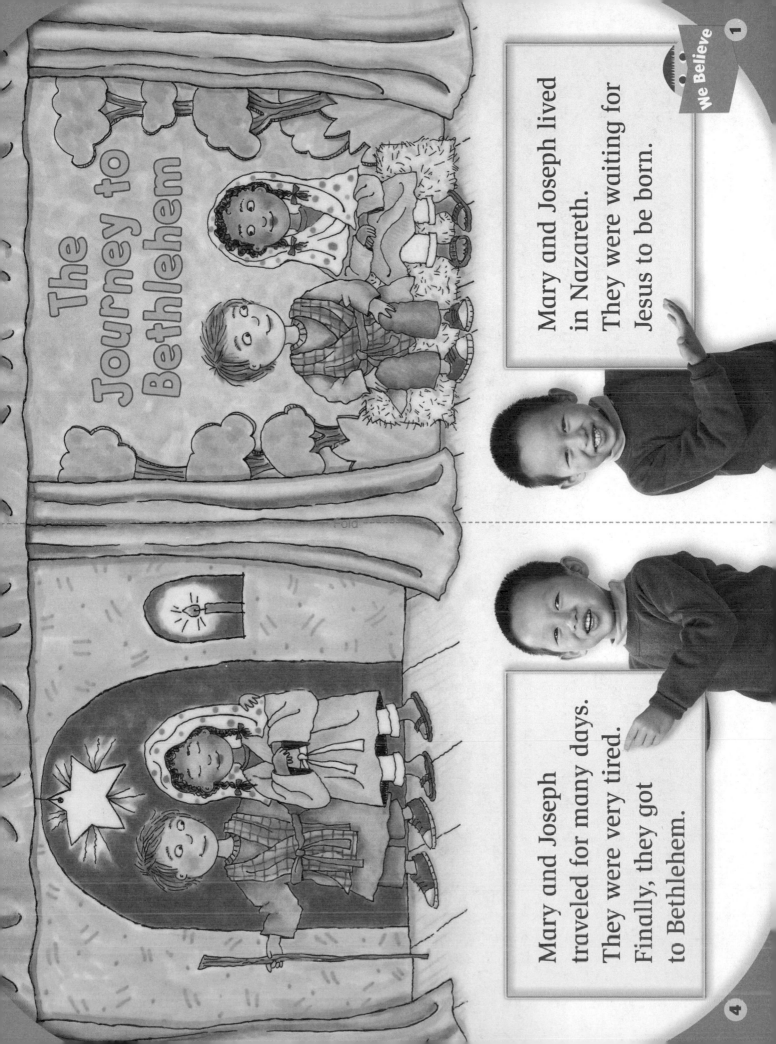

The Journey to Bethlehem

Mary and Joseph lived
in Nazareth.
They were waiting for
Jesus to be born.

Mary and Joseph
traveled for many days.
They were very tired.
Finally, they got
to Bethlehem.

The ruler wanted to
know how many people
there were in the world.
He wanted everyone
counted.

Mary and Joseph left
Nazareth.
They traveled to
Bethlehem to be counted.

Let's Celebrate
Waiting for Jesus

✝ We Pray

🎵 Advent Canon

Come, Lord Jesus,
come and save us.
Come, Lord Jesus, come.

In this season
we are waiting.
Come, Lord Jesus, come.

PROJECT DISCIPLE

Help Mary and Joseph find their way from Nazareth to Bethlehem.

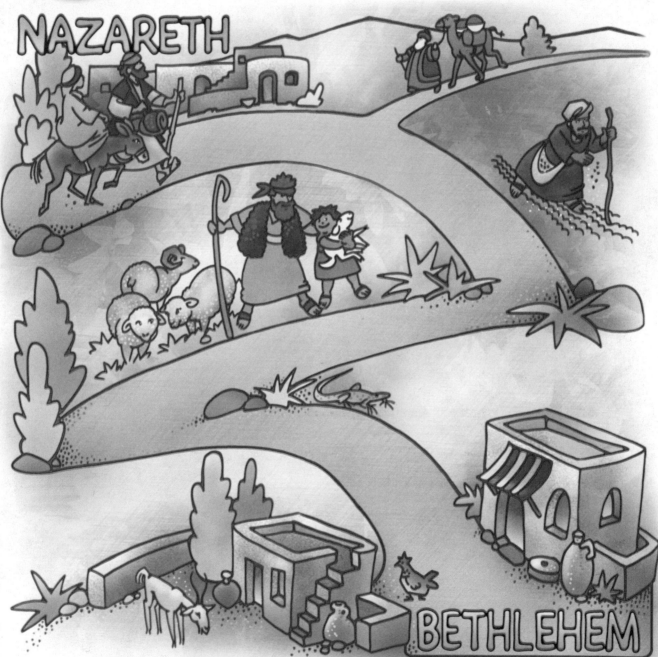

Take Home

Commemorate Advent as a family by displaying an Advent calendar. Open a door of the calendar together each day as you pray, *Come, Lord Jesus*.

Christmas

14

Advent | Christmas | Ordinary Time | Lent | Three Days | Easter | Ordinary Time

WE GATHER

"For a child is born to us,
a son is given us."

(Isaiah 9:5)

What are some special gifts
God has given to us?

Jesus was born in Bethlehem.

📖 Luke 2:1–8

Read to Me

When Mary and Joseph reached Bethlehem, they were very tired. There was no place to stay. Finally an innkeeper let them stay in the place where he kept his animals. Jesus was born there. Mary wrapped him in a cloth. She laid him in a manger that was filled with hay.

🎵 Away in a Manger

Away in a manger,
no crib for a bed,
The little Lord Jesus
laid down his
sweet head;
The stars in the sky
looked down
where he lay,
The little Lord Jesus,
asleep on the hay.

We celebrate Christmas.

Each Christmas we celebrate the birth of Jesus.
All over the world people pray and thank God for sending his Son.

Make a "Star of Bethlehem."
It will be like the bright one in the sky on the night Jesus was born.

WE RESPOND

Rejoice! Jesus is born!
We welcome you, Jesus,
each in our own way.

👤 Talk about some special things your family does for Christmas. Draw one of them here.

The Visit of the Shepherds

It was the night Jesus was born.

The shepherds went to Bethlehem to find Jesus. The shepherds were happy to find the newborn baby.

Shepherds were in a
field near Bethlehem.
They were taking care
of their sheep.

Suddenly, a bright light lit up
the sky.
Angels started to sing.
The angels told the shepherds
about Jesus.

Fold

Let's Celebrate
Christmas

♫ **Silent Night, Holy Night**

Silent night! Holy night!
All is calm, all is bright
Round yon Virgin Mother
and child!
Holy infant so tender and mild,
Sleep in heavenly peace,
Sleep in heavenly peace.

Silent night! Holy night!
Shepherds quake at the sight;
Glories stream from heaven afar;
Heav'nly hosts sing "Alleluia!
Christ the Savior is born,
Christ the Savior is born."

131

Pray
Learn
Celebrate
Share
Choose
Live

Circle the ways you can celebrate Christmas.

Take Home

What can your family learn from the many Christmas hymns about Jesus' birth?

Sacraments

Part 1   I Open My Heart

What does the word *strong* mean?
Act out what it means to be strong.

Circle what makes you feel strong.

STRONG

Sacraments

Part 2 We Come Together for Prayer

Leader: "The Lord stood by me and gave me strength." (2 Timothy 4:17)

O God, you give us strength. In the sacraments, you give us a special kind of strength. We have received the Sacrament of Baptism. You have given us the strength to be holy and to serve you in all that we do.

Reader 1: I will serve you, Lord, with my hands. (*All clap.*)

Reader 2: I will serve you, Lord, with my feet. (*All dance.*)

Reader 3: I will serve you, Lord, with my joy. (*All smile at a friend.*)

All: I will serve you, Lord, with my love. (*All join hands.*) Amen.

Sacraments

Part 3   I Cherish God's Word

"Be holy, for I, the LORD, your God, am holy."
(Leviticus 19:2)

LISTEN to the reading from Scripture. Pay close attention to the reading.

REFLECT on what you heard. Think about:

- How can you be holy as Jesus taught you to be?

SHARE your thoughts and feelings with God in prayer. Speak to God as a friend.

CONTEMPLATE or sit quietly and think about God's Word in the Scripture passage from the Book of Leviticus above.

Sacraments

Part 4   I Value My Catholic Faith

At Baptism, you became a child of God. God made you his own. You belong to God.

Listen as you hear about belonging to God, and color each part of this drawing.

All of us are children of God, and all of us are members of the Church.

Sacraments

Part 5   I Celebrate Catholic Identity

Read to Me

The sacraments are special celebrations that Jesus gave to the Church. They are: Baptism, Confirmation, Eucharist, Penance and Reconciliation, Anointing of the Sick, Holy Orders, and Matrimony.

God gives us grace in the sacraments. Grace is a special kind of strength. It is the gift of God's life in us. It helps us to be holy and follow Jesus.

Listen as you are told about each sacrament and about what you might see.

Then be a reporter. Choose one sacrament. Report to your group on what you have learned about that sacrament.

- Baptism

- Confirmation

- Eucharist

- Penance and Reconciliation

- Anointing of the Sick

- Holy Orders

- Matrimony

Sacraments

Part 6 I Honor My Catholic Identity

Reader: "Be strong in the grace that is in Christ Jesus." (2 Timothy 2:1)

Leader: O God, through the sacraments, you give us grace. You welcome us into your family. You nourish, heal, and forgive us. You help us to serve.

All: O, that your love might be the peace of my soul, the strength and happiness, the goal of my life, the whole of my heart! Amen.

(Adapted from a prayer of Saint Rose of Lima)

Saint Rose of Lima

Catholic Identity Retreat

Bringing the Retreat Home

Sacraments

Retreat Recap

Review the pages of your child's *Celebrating Catholic Identity: Liturgy & Sacraments* retreat. Ask your child to tell you about the retreat. Talk about the sacraments:

■ The sacraments are special celebrations that Jesus gave to the Church.

■ There are Seven Sacraments: Baptism, Confirmation, Eucharist, Penance and Reconciliation, Anointing of the Sick, Holy Orders, and Matrimony.

■ In the sacraments, we receive God's grace, God's life in us, which strengthens us and makes us holy.

Images of the Sacraments

In this retreat, your child explored what we see in the sacraments, such as water, oil, bread, and wine. Have your child decide which sacrament he or she would like to draw a picture of. Talk about what was included in his or her drawing.

Take a Moment

Talk to your child about the sacraments that he or she and other members of your family have received. If you have photos or videos of these special celebrations, look at them together.

Family Prayer

Pray these words as a mealtime prayer.

O God, who constantly feed and strengthen the Church
with your Sacraments,
grant to us, . . .
that, by obeying your teachings of love,
we may become for the human family
a life-giving leaven and a means to salvation.
Through Christ our Lord. Amen.

(Prayer after Communion, Mass for the Church)

For more resources, see the *Catholic Identity Home Companion* at the end of this book.

Why We Believe
As a Catholic Family

What if someone asks us:

- What does the Catholic Church teach about sacraments?

The following resources can help us to respond:

The Church celebrates Seven Sacraments: Baptism, Eucharist, Confirmation, Penance and Reconciliation, Anointing of the Sick, Holy Orders, and Matrimony.

The Seven Sacraments are effective signs because they truly bring about what they celebrate. For example, in Baptism we not only celebrate being children of God, we actually become children of God. In Penance and Reconciliation we not only celebrate that God forgives, we actually receive God's forgiveness.

Jesus instituted, or began, the sacraments so that his saving work would continue for all time. A sacrament is an effective sign given to us by Jesus Christ through which we share in God's life—grace. The grace that we receive in the sacraments is called *sanctifying grace*.

🌿 What does Scripture say?

Jesus said, "Go, therefore, and make disciples of all nations, baptizing them in the name of the Father, and of the Son, and of the holy Spirit" (Matthew 28:19).

"Then [Jesus] took the bread, said the blessing, broke it, and gave it to them, saying, 'This is my body, which will be given for you; do this in memory of me.' And likewise the cup after they had eaten, saying, 'This cup is the new covenant in my blood, which will be shed for you.'" (Luke 22:19–20)

The sacraments unite all Catholics with Jesus and with one another. The priest and other members of the Church who participate in the sacraments represent the whole Church. The Seven Sacraments are the most important celebrations of the Church.

🌿 What does the Church say?

"*The seven sacraments are the signs and instruments by which the Holy Spirit spreads the grace of Christ the head throughout the Church which is his Body.*" (CCC, 774)

"*The purpose of the sacraments is to sanctify men, to build up the body of Christ, and, finally, to give worship to God.*" (Constitution on the Sacred Liturgy, Second Vatican Council, 59)

"*[No one must say that the sacraments] were not all instituted by Jesus Christ, our Lord; or, that they are more, or less, than seven . . . or even that any one of these seven is not truly and properly a sacrament.*" (Council of Trent, Seventh Session)

Notes:

Jesus Shows Us God's Love

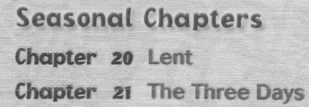

Seasonal Chapters

PROJECT DISCIPLE
DEAR FAMILY

In Unit 3 your child will grow as a disciple of Jesus by:

- appreciating Mary's role in God's plan
- understanding that God the Father showed his love by sending Jesus
- learning about the Holy Family and praying to them
- listening to Jesus' teachings
- being kind, good, caring, and loving as Jesus was.

What Would *you* do?

Jesus wants us to show others that we love them. Decide on one way your family will show love for:

Neighbors _____

People in your parish _____

Workers _____

Each other _____

Pray Today

One way we can honor Mary is by praying to her. The Hail Mary is on page 141 of your child's text. Ask your child to teach the prayer gestures to your family. Pray the Hail Mary as a family each day for a week.

Reality Check

"The Christian family is a communion of persons, a sign and image of the communion of the Father and the Son in the Holy Spirit."

(*Catechism of the Catholic Church*, 2205)

What's *the* Word?

Ask your child to share what he or she is learning about Jesus and his teachings. Then invite each family member to share a favorite Scripture story of Jesus. You might refer to a children's Bible as each person shares his or her favorite.

More *to* Explore

As your child learns about Jesus and his family, use a globe or world map to find the places Jesus lived or visited. Look for Bethlehem, Nazareth, and Jerusalem. Then choose one of these cities to research further and discover what that place is like today.

Take Home

Each chapter in your child's *We Believe* Kindergarten text offers a "Take Home" activity that invites your family to support your child's journey to more fully become a disciple of Christ.

Be ready for this unit's Take Home:

Chapter 15: Honoring Mary at home and church

Chapter 16: Learning about Jesus in the Bible

Chapter 17: Comparing your own family with the Holy Family

Chapter 18: Acting like Jesus

Chapter 19: Sharing love as a family

God Chooses Mary

WE GATHER

📖 Luke 1:28

God is with you.

A Child Is Born, © 2014 Michael Escoffery/Artists Rights Society (ARS), New York

Martin and his dad are looking at a special picture.

What does the picture show?

Mary loved God very much.

There was a young Jewish
girl named Mary.
She lived with her family
in the town of Nazareth.
Mary showed her love for God.
She helped other people.
Mary prayed every day.

How do you think Mary helped
her mother? Act it out.

God asked Mary to be the Mother of his Son.

📖 Luke 1:26–31

Read Along

One day an angel brought Mary a message from God. God wanted Mary to be the Mother of his Son. God wanted her to name the child Jesus.

Mary wanted to do what God asked.

What did Mary say to God?

Mary's answer to God is hiding in these letters.

🏃 Circle it.

M G Y E S D Q

WE RESPOND

We can show our love for God, too.
This is how we say **yes** to God.
We can pray.
We can work and play together.
We can help others.

Draw a picture to show how you can say **yes** to God.

We Honor Mary

Jesus told us that Mary is our mother. So people all over the world honor Mary. Mary is the greatest of all saints.

We honor Mary at home.

We can honor Mary
in many ways.
When we honor Mary,
we honor Jesus, too.

We honor Mary in
our churches.

2

3

Fold

Let's Celebrate
Mary

✝ **We Pray**

Hail Mary, full of grace,
the Lord is with you!

(Raise arms over head.)

Blessed are you among women,
and blessed is the fruit of
   your womb, Jesus.

(Cross arms over heart.)

Holy Mary, Mother of God,
pray for us sinners,

(Put arms down at sides with
palms facing front.)

now and at the hour
   of our death.
Amen.

(Join palms of hands together
to form prayer position.)

141

Pray Learn Celebrate Share Choose Live

Who is the Mother of God's Son?
Trace the letters.
Color the picture.

Mary

Tell a friend what Mary said to God.

Take Home

Discuss ways you can honor Mary at home and at church.
Decide on one way your family will honor Mary this week.

God the Father Gives Us Jesus

16

WE GATHER

"For God so loved the world that he gave his only Son."
(John 3:16)

What do you give to the people you love?

Jesus is the Son of God.

God is our loving Father.
He loves us very much.
God gives us many gifts.
His greatest gift to us is his Son.
Jesus is God's only Son.

Color every space that has a ♡.
Whose name do you see?

Jesus is one of us.

Jesus was born a long time ago.
He was a baby just as we were.
He grew up.
He had many feelings,
just as we do.

🧍 What do you think Jesus
did when he was your age?
Draw what you think he did.

Looking at the Sun

WE RESPOND

What stories about Jesus do you know?
What is your favorite story?

Look at the pictures.
They show ways people learn about Jesus.
Color the bows by the pictures of ways you learn about Jesus.

A Package from Grandpa

Look what came today! It's a package from Grandpa. He wrote some clues to help us guess what it is.

Fold

Let's open the package. What do you think it is? Oh! It's a Bible!

THE CATHOLIC BIBLE

THE CATH

Let's Celebrate
God's Gift of Jesus

✝ **We Pray**

🎵 **Jesus in the Morning**

Jesus, Jesus,
Jesus in the morning,
Jesus at the noontime;
Jesus, Jesus,
Jesus when the sun goes down!

Thank him, Thank him,
Thank him in the morning,
Thank him at the noontime;
Thank him, Thank him,
Thank him when the sun
goes down!

PROJECT DISCIPLE

God's greatest gift to us is his Son.
Draw him here.

- - - - - - - Jesus - - - - - - -

www.webelieveweb.com

Take Home

Discuss what you can learn about Jesus from Bible stories that you know. Finish with a prayer thanking God for the gift of Jesus, his only Son.

150   Kindergarten   Chapter 16

Jesus Grew Up in Nazareth

WE GATHER

"The child grew and became strong." (Luke 2:40)

How do you grow and become strong? Who helps you to do this?

Jesus grew up in a family.

Mary was Jesus' mother. Joseph was his foster father.

Jesus, Mary, and Joseph are called the Holy Family.

🏃 Draw a ✔ next to the pictures of the things you can do with your family.

Jesus, Mary, and Joseph showed their love for one another.

The Holy Family lived in Nazareth. Mary and Joseph helped Jesus learn many things. Jesus helped them in their work.

Find what Jesus helped Joseph to make. Connect the dots and color.

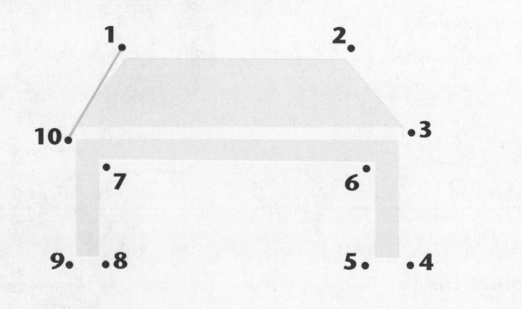

Find what Jesus helped Mary to make. Connect the dots and color.

WE RESPOND

The Holy Family showed their love for God and one another. How can your family do what the Holy Family did?

🏃 Match.

The Holy Family	Your Family
prayed to God everyday	
shared stories about God and his people	
helped one another learn about God's world	

Jesus in the Temple

Luke 2:41–51

Jesus' family went to Jerusalem. They went there to worship God in the Temple. A special feast was being celebrated.

Fold

Finally they found Jesus in the Temple. He was talking to the people about God. Everyone was amazed at how much Jesus knew.

4

When the celebration was over, Mary and Joseph left. Mary thought Jesus was with Joseph. Joseph thought Jesus was with Mary.

Later Mary and Joseph could not find Jesus. They were very upset. They returned to Jerusalem. They searched the city for their son.

Fold

Let's Celebrate
The Holy Family

✝ **We Pray**

Holy Family, we ask you this day,

- to help us at work
- to help us at play
- to help us at school
- to help us at home
- to help us care for others
- to help us _____.

Holy Family, help us be like you in every way.

PROJECT DISCIPLE

Tell what the Holy Family is doing in each picture.

Draw a way your family does one of these activities.

Take Home

Use the drawing from the completed Project Disciple activity above to discuss ways your own family is like the Holy Family.

Jesus Teaches and Helps Us

WE GATHER

📖 Matthew 4:23

Jesus went everywhere teaching and helping people.

Look at the picture.
How do people help and teach you in each of these places?

School

Library +Hospital+ GROCERY BARBER

EMERGENCY SALE

STOP

159

WE BELIEVE

Jesus taught many people.

When Jesus was a grown-up,
he left his home in Nazareth.

📖 Matthew 4:23–25

Read Along

Jesus went to many places. Many people listened
to Jesus as he taught about God. People who were
sick, poor, or hungry went to Jesus for help.

Wherever Jesus went, people
came to see him.

Where did Jesus go?
Follow the path to see.
Talk about each place along the way.

160

Jesus was kind, good, and caring.

Jesus helped people who were sick.
Jesus talked to people.
He listened to them.

📖 Luke 18:15–16

Read Along

Jesus had been teaching all day. People were bringing their children so he could bless them. When Jesus' friends saw this, they tried to stop the people. But Jesus said, "Let the children come to me."

🧍 Draw yourself with Jesus.

🎵 Jesus Wants to Help Us

We believe Jesus wants to help us.
We believe Jesus wants to help us.
We believe that Jesus always
  wants to help us.

Ev'ry day Jesus is beside us.
Ev'ry day Jesus is beside us.
We believe that Jesus always
  is beside us.

JESUS JESUS

Loaves and Fish

📖 John 6:3–15

One day thousands of people were listening to Jesus teach. Jesus saw that it was getting late. He knew that the people were hungry.

Fold

Everyone in the crowd had plenty to eat. People were amazed at what Jesus did. They praised and thanked him.

Jesus asked his friends
to find some food.
They found a boy who
had five loaves of bread
and two fish.

Fold

Jesus blessed the
bread and fish.
He gave thanks to God.
Jesus told his friends
to hand out the food.

Let's Celebrate

Jesus

✝ **We Pray**

📖 Luke 18:16

Jesus, you said, "Let the children come to me."

Today we come to you in prayer. Jesus, we thank you for your love. We pray for all the children of the world. We know that you will always help us. Amen.

Jesus helped people.
Jesus helps us.

Decorate this thank-you card for Jesus.

Thank you Jesus!

Take Home

Remember some of the things that Jesus did for others.
Which of these things can your family do this week?

Jesus Wants Us to Love

WE GATHER

Jesus said,
"Love one another as I
love you" (John 15:12).

Imagine you are in the crowd.
What do you hear Jesus saying?

Jesus wants us to tell others we love them.

We can tell other people we love them by the words we say. Sometimes we say, "I love you." Sometimes we can use other words.

How do you feel?

I am sorry.

Color around the words that we say to those we love.

Can I help you?

Jesus wants us to show others we love them.

Jesus wants us to be kind.
Jesus wants us to share.
Jesus wants us to be fair.
Jesus wants us to listen to one another.

Look at the picture. Circle the people who are doing what Jesus wants us to do.

WE RESPOND

We can ask Jesus
to help us love others.
Ask Jesus to help
you today.

Draw yourself showing love to others.

Saint John Bosco

Saint John Bosco grew up in a poor family in Italy. He helped his family by doing different jobs.

Fold

John started schools where young people learned to do different jobs.
He built places for them to work.
John's kindness showed the young people how to love God and others.

4

John wanted to tell people
about God.
So he learned how to juggle.
When people came to
watch him, John told them
about God's love.

Fold

When John was older,
he became a priest.
He helped many poor
and homeless children.
He found places for them
to live, work, and pray.

Let's Celebrate
God's Gift of Love

✝ **We Pray**

🎵 **Listen to Jesus**

Alleluia, alleluia,
    alleluia, alleluia!
Listen to Jesus.
Do what he tells you.

Open your hearts today.

Live in God's love today.

Pray
Learn
Celebrate
Share
Choose
Live

Color the spaces with ♥ red .
Color the picture.

What does Jesus want us to do?

Take Home

Talk about ways your family members show love to each other. Then discuss how it makes each of you feel to show love and to receive love.

Lent

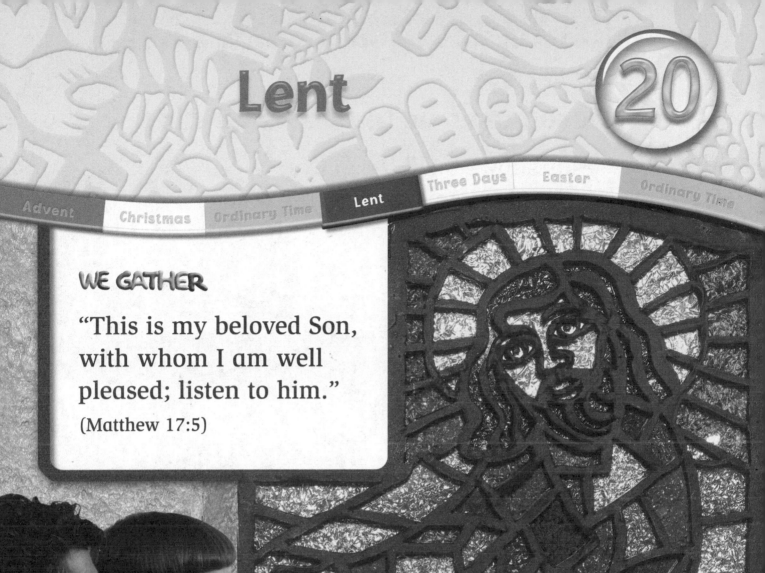

WE GATHER

"This is my beloved Son, with whom I am well pleased; listen to him."
(Matthew 17:5)

When do you listen to Jesus?

175

Jesus asks us to live as he did.

Jesus showed us how to live.
He wants us to love God and others.
There is a special time of year when we
try to do this.

176

We celebrate Lent.

During this special time we pray.
We try to act as Jesus did.
We find ways to care for others.

Jesus cared for everyone.
Many people care for you.
You can care for them, too.

Act out a way you can show them you care.

A Special Time for Jesus

We learn about Jesus.

Fold

We help others as Jesus did.

We celebrate that
Jesus loves us.

We love
others as
Jesus did.

Fold

2

3

Let's Celebrate
Our Friend Jesus

✝ **We Pray**

🎵 **I Am Your Friend**

Chorus
I am your friend,
always here beside you,
to watch and be with you
in all that you do.
I am your friend,
I am your friend.

Jesus helps us ev'ry day
in the fears that come our way,
in our hearts we hear him say: (Chorus)

PROJECT DISCIPLE

Color the shapes next to the pictures that show people celebrating Lent.

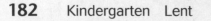
Take Home

During Lent families can make a special effort to care for each other. Discuss ways the members of your family can care for each other.

WE GATHER

"For God so loved the world."

(John 3:16)

What days are very important to you?

The Three Days are very special.

Jesus loved us so much!
He gave his whole life for us.
We celebrate this in a special way
on the Three Days known as the
Easter Triduum.

We celebrate the Three Days.

Thank Jesus for his love.

 Write your name on the banner.

Draw a picture to show that you love Jesus.

The Greatest Days

We celebrate three
great days.
We pray and show
God our love.

Fold

We celebrate that
Jesus loves us.
Alleluia!

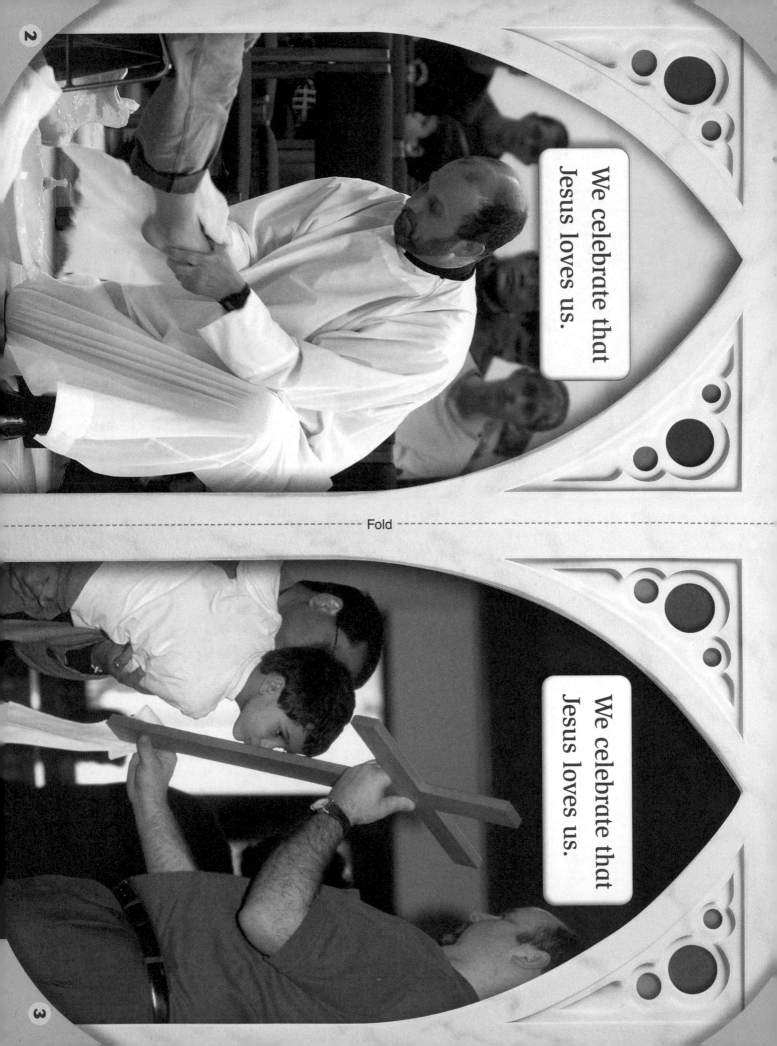

We celebrate that Jesus loves us.

Fold

We celebrate that Jesus loves us.

Let's Celebrate

The Three Days

✝ **We Pray**

🎵 **Sing for Joy**

Sing and jump for joy, alleluia!
Sing and jump for joy, alleluia!
Sing and jump for joy, alleluia!
Alleluia! Alleluia!

Sing and dance for joy, alleluia!
Sing and dance for joy, alleluia!
Sing and dance for joy, alleluia!
Alleluia! Alleluia!

Pray
Learn
Celebrate
Share
Choose
Live

The cross is decorated with flowers.
Color the flowers to show that the
Three Days are very special.

Take Home

Discuss ways that your family can demonstrate love for
Jesus. As a family pray, *Jesus, thank you for loving us. We
love you.*

Loving Others

Part 1   I Open My Heart

Think about someone you love. Tell about one way you show love to that person.

Then color the picture that shows loving others.

Loving Others

Part 2   **We Come Together for Prayer**

Leader: "God is love." (1 John 4:8) God, we feel your love in many ways. Thank you for your gift of love. Hold hands as we sing.

🎵 **The Gifts of God's Love**

("*Did You Ever See a Lassie?*")

Let's celebrate together, together, together.
Let's celebrate together
God's great love for us.

God gives us our families.
He gives us our good friends.
Let's celebrate together
The gifts of God's love.

Leader: God, your greatest gift of love was sending your Son, Jesus. Jesus shows us your love.

Reader 1: God, we celebrate your love!

Reader 2: God, we celebrate the love of Jesus!

Reader 3: God, we celebrate the love of our families and friends!

All: Amen.

Loving Others

Part 3 I Cherish God's Word

Jesus said, "Love one another as I love you" (John 15:12).

LISTEN to the reading from Scripture. Pay close attention to the reading.

REFLECT on what you heard. Think about:

- How Jesus loves us.

- How can you love others?

SHARE your thoughts and feelings with God in prayer. Speak to God as a friend.

CONTEMPLATE or sit quietly and think about God's Word in the Scripture passage from the Gospel of John above.

Loving Others

Part 4   I Value My Catholic Faith

Jesus, God the Son, teaches us to love God the Father and to love one another. This kind of love moves us to action!

Work with a partner to make a handprint heart.

"Helping Hands Make Loving Hearts"

Loving Others

Part 5   I Celebrate Catholic Identity

Jesus wants you to love all people. Below, draw one way you can love others.

Catholic Identity Retreat

Loving Others

Part 6 I Honor My Catholic Identity

Leader: Dear Jesus, you said, "You are the light of the world"(Matthew 5:14).

Imagine the light of Jesus' love in your heart. Think about the light of this love as we sing:

🎵 **This Little Light of Mine**

This little light of mine, I'm gonna
let it shine.
This little light of mine, I'm gonna
let it shine.
This little light of mine,*

*I'm gonna let it shine.
Let it shine, let it shine, let it shine.

Ev'rywhere I go, I'm gonna let it shine.
Ev'rywhere I go, I'm gonna let it shine.
Ev'rywhere I go,*

Jesus gave it to me; I'm gonna let it shine.
Jesus gave it to me; I'm gonna let it shine.
Jesus gave it to me;*

Catholic Identity Retreat

Bringing the Retreat Home

Loving Others

Retreat Recap

Review the pages of your child's *Celebrating Catholic Identity: Morality* retreat. Ask your child to tell you about the retreat. Talk about loving others:

- God loves us.
- Jesus, God the Son, shows us God the Father's love and teaches us to love God and others.
- We are called to love others as Jesus loves us.

Family Love

Make a list of the ways your family can show love for one another using the letters of the word *LOVE*. Color the letters together.

Take a Moment

In your child's retreat, he or she made a heart using handprints with another child. Make a series of hearts on drawing paper using all of your family's handprints with washable paints in various colors. Label each person's handprint with his or her name. Talk about ways your family can lend a helping hand to others as a sign of love.

Family Prayer

Pray together an Act of Love at bedtime.

O God, we love you above all things. Help us to love ourselves and one another as Jesus taught us to do.

For more resources, see the *Catholic Identity Home Companion* at the end of this book.

Catholic Identity Retreat

Why We Believe
As a Catholic Family

What if someone asks us:

- What is Catholic moral teaching based on?

The following resources can help us to respond:

Catholic moral teaching has its foundation in Scripture.

🌿 What does Scripture say?

- Ten Commandments (see Exodus 20:1–17)
- Beatitudes (see Matthew 5:1–12)
- Great Commandment (see Matthew 22:37–39)
- New Commandment (see John 13:34–35)

Catholic social teaching flows from all of the above. Jesus treated all people equally and respected the dignity of every person. As his disciples, we too are called to choose actions that show our love for God, others, and ourselves.

Catholic moral teaching guides us in making decisions between right and wrong. Catholic moral teaching has its basis in the inherent dignity of every person: that is, that each of us is made in the image of God. By showing love and respect for God, ourselves, and one another, we are following Catholic moral teaching.

Catholic moral teaching also has its foundation in the teachings of the Church.

🌿 What does the Church say?

"The Word of God is a light for our path. We must assimilate it in faith and prayer and put it into practice. This is how moral conscience is formed." (CCC, 1802)

"Deep within his conscience man discovers a law which he has not laid upon himself but which he must obey. Its voice, ever calling him to love and to do what is good and to avoid evil, sounds in his heart at the right moment. . . . For man has in his heart a law inscribed by God. . . . His conscience is man's most secret core and his sanctuary. There he is alone with God whose voice echoes in his depths." (*Gaudium et Spes*, 16, as quoted in CCC, 1776)

Notes:

Jesus Wants Us to Share God's Love

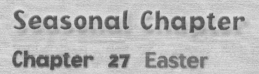

DEAR FAMILY

In Unit 4 your child will grow as a disciple of Jesus by:

- recognizing that through Baptism we belong to God's family, the Church
- praying as Jesus did
- celebrating with the Church at Mass
- learning ways we can show our love for God and others
- appreciating Jesus as our friend.

Make it Happen

At the end of Mass, the priest dismisses us. Talk about what your family will do after Mass on Sunday to love and serve the Lord and others.

Celebrate!

Tell your child about his or her Baptism. Share any mementos you have: photos, videos, Baptismal candle, white garment. Consider sharing your own Baptism story, too. Where were you baptized? by whom? Contact your own and your child's godparents—by letter, card, e-mail, or phone.

Reality Check

"The family should live in such a way that its members learn to care and take responsibility for the young, the old, the sick, the handicapped, and the poor."

(*Catechism of the Catholic Church*, 2208)

Fast Facts

According to the 2009 Pontifical Year-book, there were 1.147 billion Catholics worldwide at the end of 2007. A 2007 census showed there were 67 million Catholics in the United States. Help your child to appreciate how many people throughout the world share our faith!

Pray Today

Begin teaching your child the simple responses we say at Mass to help him or her participate. Use the *We Pray at Mass* booklet your child makes in Chapter 24.

Take Home

Each chapter in your child's *We Believe* Kindergarten text offers a "Take Home" activity that invites your family to support your child's journey to more fully become a disciple of Christ.

Be ready for this unit's Take Home:

Chapter 22: Praying the Sign of the Cross

Chapter 23: Integrating prayer into family life

Chapter 24: Celebrating at Mass

Chapter 25: Caring for others

Chapter 26: Remembering that Jesus is always with your family

We Belong to the Church

WE GATHER

📖 1 John 3:1

See what love the Father has given us. "We may be called the children of God."

Look at the people in each place. Why are they together?

193

The Church is the family of God.

God loves us very much.
He wants each of us to be part
of his family.
God's special family is the Church.
The Church is all over the world.

Draw your family as part of
God's family.

At Baptism we become members of the Church.

Baptism is the beginning of our new life in God's family. Look at the picture. At Baptism the priest or deacon says these words while he pours the water.

"____, I baptize you in the name of the Father, and of the Son, and of the Holy Spirit."

🏃 Water is a sign of life. Color this sign of life.

WE RESPOND

You were baptized.
You were welcomed into the Church.
The priest or deacon poured
water over you.
He said,

"_____

- -

_____

(name)

I baptize you in the name of the Father,
and of the Son,
and of the Holy Spirit."

Put a picture of your Baptism here.

The Sign of the Cross

We can learn a
special prayer.
It is called the
Sign of the Cross.
We can pray it
anywhere.

Fold

Pray the Sign of the Cross.
Pray it often.

4

1. In the name
of the Father,

2. and of the Son,

Here is the way we pray
the Sign of the Cross.

---- Fold ----

3. and of the Holy

5. Amen.

4. Spirit.

Let's Celebrate
Belonging to the Church

✝ **We Pray**

🎵 **God Is a Part of My Life**

God is a part of my life.
God is a part of my life.
God is a part of my life.
I rejoice, I rejoice, I rejoice.

I am a part of God's life!
I am a part of God's life!
I am a part, I belong to
God's family.
I am a part of God's life!

PROJECT DISCIPLE

Pray
Learn
Celebrate
Share
Choose
Live

Trace the numbers next to each part of the prayer.
Pray the Sign of the Cross.

1

2

3

4

5

Take Home

Pray as a family, *God, thank you for inviting us into your family.* Begin and end with the Sign of the Cross.

We Pray As Jesus Did

WE GATHER

📖 Jeremiah 29:12

When you pray to me, I will listen.

Look at the pictures.

What is the same?
What is different?

WE BELIEVE

Prayer is one way we can show our love for God.

Prayer is listening to and talking to God.
We can pray to God anytime.
We can pray to him anywhere.
We can talk to God about anything we want.

Draw a picture of yourself praying.

WE BELIEVE

Jesus showed us how to pray.

In the Bible we can read about Jesus praying. He prayed everywhere:

- with his family and friends
- outdoors
- at celebrations
- in holy places.

Jesus wants us to pray, too.

We can pray by ourselves. We can pray with other people. Put a ✔ next to the pictures that show where you pray with others.

Here is a prayer that Jesus taught us.

The Lord's Prayer

Our Father, who art in heaven,
hallowed be thy name;
thy kingdom come;
thy will be done on earth
    as it is in heaven.
Give us this day our daily bread;
and forgive us our trespasses
as we forgive those
    who trespass against us;
and lead us not into temptation,
but deliver us from evil. Amen.

Color in the name of this prayer.

God, I Love to Talk to You

God, when I was little, someone helped me to pray.

Fold

Thank you, God, for all you do.

Now that I can pray myself,
there are many things
I want to say.

Fold

God, bless my family
and my friends.
Bless the people who
are hungry or sick.
Please keep us all
close to you.

Let's Celebrate
Praying to God

✝ **We Pray**

Alleluia is a joyful prayer
to God.

🎵 **Sing for Joy**

Sing and shout for joy, alleluia!
Sing and shout for joy, alleluia!
Sing and shout for joy, alleluia!
Alleluia! Alleluia!

Sing and clap your hands, alleluia!
Sing and clap your hands, alleluia!
Sing and clap your hands, alleluia!
Alleluia! Alleluia!

Sing and jump for joy, alleluia!
Sing and jump for joy, alleluia!
Sing and jump for joy, alleluia!
Alleluia! Alleluia!

PROJECT DISCIPLE

Listen to the story.
Color the picture.

Read Along
Saint Kateri Tekakwitha was a Native American.
She taught children prayers.
She shared stories about Jesus.
Kateri prayed, "Jesus, I love you."

Take Home

Integrate prayer into your family's daily life. Pray at meals,
pray to begin and end the day, and pray always in moments
of joy and sorrow.

We Celebrate Jesus' Gift of Himself

WE GATHER

Jesus said, "Take this and share it" (Luke 22:17).

Act out what people say and do at celebrations.

Jesus shared a special meal with his friends, the Apostles.

Jack Savitsky, **artist** *Last Supper*

We call this special meal the Last Supper.
At this meal Jesus prayed with his Apostles.
Together they thanked God.
Jesus blessed bread and wine.
This bread and wine became the Body
and Blood of Jesus.

Jesus gave the gift of himself at the

LAST SUPPER

Jesus shares himself with us, too.

The Mass is a special celebration.
We thank God for his gifts.
We remember Jesus in a special way.
At Mass the priest blesses bread and wine.
The bread and wine become the Body and Blood of Jesus.

👤 Jesus gives us the gift of himself at

MASS

Think about the many gifts
God has given to you.
Thank him by singing.

♫ Celebrate God

Chorus
Celebrate God with your hands.
Celebrate God with your voice.
Celebrate God in all that you do.
And God will be with you.

Listen to God with your mind.
Listen to God in your heart.
Listen to God speaking with you.
And God will be with you. (Chorus)

We Pray at Mass

At Mass we thank and praise God.
We sing songs together.
We sing, "Glory to God."

The priest blesses us.
He tells us to love God and others.
We say, "Thanks be to God."

Fold

The priest or deacon reads to us about Jesus. We listen carefully. We say, **"Praise to you, Lord Jesus Christ."**

Fold

The priest prays over the bread and wine. The bread and wine become the Body and Blood of Jesus. Together we remember what Jesus has done. The priest prays and thanks God. We sing, **"Amen."**

Let's Celebrate
Jesus' Gift of Himself

✝ **We Pray**

Thank you, Jesus, for sharing yourself with us.
Jesus, we thank you.

Thank you, Jesus, for the gift of yourself at Mass.
Jesus, we thank you.

Thank you, Jesus, for being with us always.
Jesus, we thank you.

PROJECT DISCIPLE

Pray
Learn
Celebrate
Share
Choose
Live

What are the people in the picture doing?

Add yourself to the picture.

Take Home

Discuss the things we do at Mass including thanking God for his gifts, remembering Jesus, singing songs, and listening to stories about Jesus. Attend a family Mass and notice all the ways people celebrate.

We Care About Others As Jesus Did

WE GATHER

Jesus said,
"As I have done for you, you should also do" (John 13:15).

How can you help others?

WE BELIEVE
Jesus cared about everyone.

Jesus fed people who were hungry.
Jesus helped people who were poor or sick.
Jesus made those who were sad or
lonely feel better.
Jesus showed us how to care for everyone.

Color the path Jesus walked.
Circle the people whom Jesus helped.

WE BELIEVE

Jesus wants us to care about others, too.

Jesus wants us to help people who are in need.

Jesus wants us to help people who are poor, sick, or lonely.

How can you show you care for someone?

Match to show what you can do.

219

There are many ways to show
we care about others.
Think about someone you know.
How can you show you care?

♫ Caring for Others
("Mary Had a Little Lamb")

Jesus cares for everyone,
everyone, everyone.
We can care for everyone
just as Jesus did.

When we help, we show we care,
show we care, show we care.
When we give, we show
    we care
just as Jesus did.

The Caring Man

📖 See Luke 10:29–37.

Jesus told this story.
One day a man was walking
down a road.
Robbers came along.
They beat him and
took his money.
They left him hurt
and alone.

Who was the caring
man in this story?
How did he show
that he cared?

Fold

4

Some people walked by
the man who was hurt.
But they did not stop to
help him.

Fold

Later, another man came
walking down the road.
He stopped and helped
the man who was hurt.

Let's Celebrate

Caring as Jesus Did

✝ **We Pray**

Jesus, you helped others.
Jesus, help us to be like you.

Jesus, you cared for others.
Jesus, help us to be like you.

Jesus, you _____.
Jesus, help us to be like you.

PROJECT DISCIPLE

Pray Learn Celebrate Share Choose Live

Draw a ✔ next to the pictures that show children caring for others.

Which is your favorite picture?

www.webelieveweb.com

Take Home

Brainstorm ways your family can help care for others. Try to do five good deeds. Once you have met your goal, have a family celebration.

We Celebrate That Jesus Is Our Friend

WE GATHER

📖 John 15:15

Jesus told us that he calls us friends.

How do you spend time with your friends?

WE BELIEVE

Jesus had many friends.

Jesus liked to spend time with his friends. Here is a story about one of those times.

📖 John 21:4–13

Read Along

One morning Jesus' friends were on a boat fishing. They looked up. They saw a man standing on the shore. Someone shouted that it was Jesus. The friends hurried to get to the shore. Jesus had fish and bread ready for them. Jesus said to his friends, "Come, have breakfast." (John 21:12) The friends sat down and ate with Jesus.

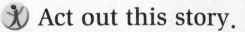 Act out this story.

WE BELIEVE

Jesus shares his friendship with us.

Jesus said,
"I am with you always" (Matthew 28:20).

Jesus is with us when we are by ourselves.
He is with us when we are with our families.
He is with us when we are with our friends.
Jesus is always with us.

I am with you always.

🏃 What does your friend Jesus say to you?
Color the words of the message.

WE RESPOND

How can you thank Jesus for being your friend?

Pray.

Be kind.

Help others.

Share.

Be fair.

Color the shells to show what you will do.

228

Always with Us

Bubbles float away.

But Jesus is with us always.

Fold

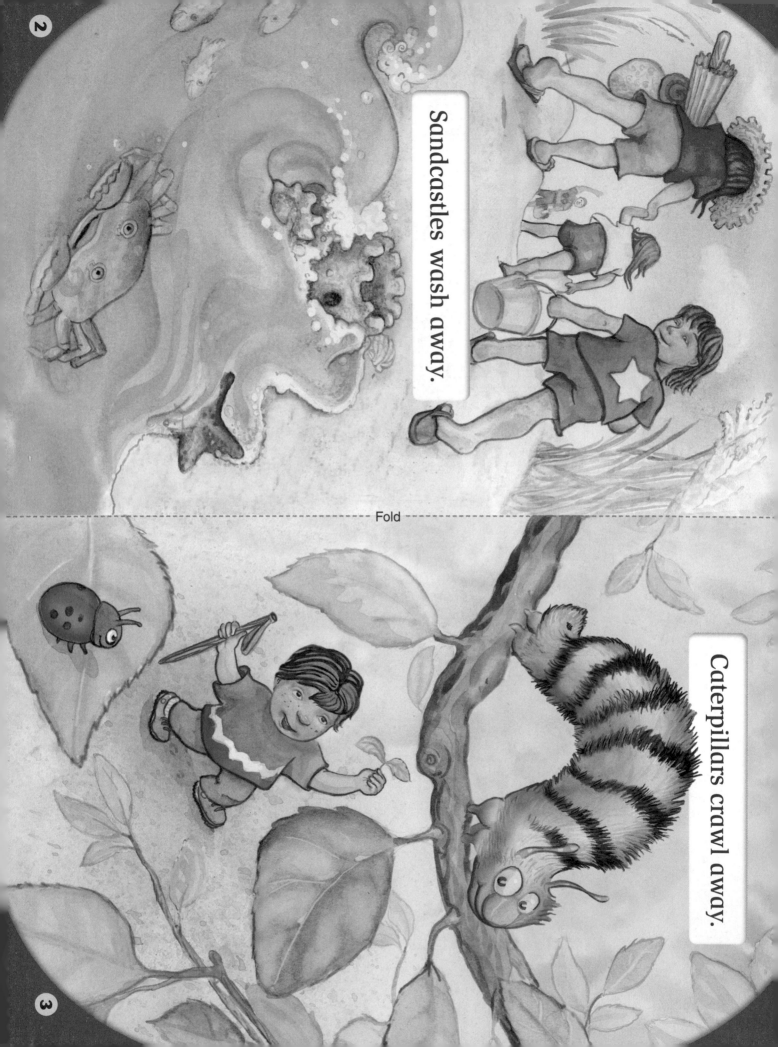

Sandcastles wash away.

Caterpillars crawl away.

Let's Celebrate

Jesus Is Our Friend

✝ **We Pray**

🎵 **Jesus in the Morning**

Jesus, Jesus,
Jesus in the morning,
Jesus at the noontime.
Jesus, Jesus,
Jesus when the sun goes down!

Love him, love him,
love him in the morning,
Love him at the noontime.
Love him, love him,
love him when the sun goes down!

PROJECT DISCIPLE

Pray
Learn
Celebrate
Share
Choose
Live

Color the spaces with 1 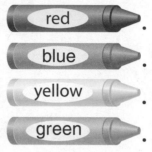 red.

Color the spaces with 2 blue.

Color the spaces with 3 yellow.

Color the spaces with 4 green.

When is Jesus with us? Tell a friend.

Take Home

Discuss times when you might feel lonely, sad, or in need of a friend. Discuss ways that Jesus can help during those times. Remember that Jesus is always with your family!

Easter

Advent · Christmas · Ordinary Time · Lent · Three Days · Easter · Ordinary Time

WE GATHER

"Sing to the LORD a new song."

(Psalm 149:1)

What does this picture make you think of?

233

We celebrate Jesus' new life.

Jesus is so wonderful.
We celebrate his love and his life.

What signs of life do you see around you? Draw some here.

We celebrate Easter.

We celebrate Jesus' new life.
We give thanks for the new life Jesus brings us.

🏃 Color the word to complete the sentence.

We celebrate new life together during

Easter.

WE RESPOND

Think about ways families celebrate Easter.

 Draw your family and friends celebrating Easter.

We Celebrate New Life

Alleluia!

Fold

Alleluia! Alleluia! Alleluia!

Alleluia!

Alleluia!

Fold

Let's Celebrate

Easter

✝ **We Pray**

🎵 **Sing a New Song**

Sing a new song unto the Lord;
let your song be sung
from mountains high.
Sing a new song unto the Lord,
singing alleluia.

PROJECT DISCIPLE

Pray Learn Celebrate Share Choose Live

Trace the message
Decorate the Easter poster
with signs of life.

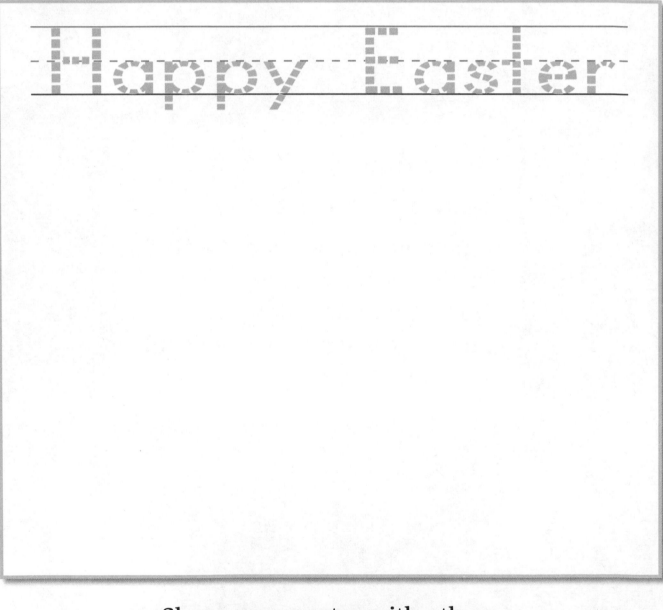

Happy Easter

Share your poster with others.

Take Home

With your family, plant and nurture a seed with soil, water, and sunlight. Watch it grow and let it remind your family to celebrate the new life of Jesus.

Praying for Others

Part 1   I Open My Heart

Imagine that you are at the park, blowing bubbles with your friends. In each large bubble, draw someone you want to talk to God about.

Catholic Identity Retreat

Praying for Others

Part 2   We Come Together for Prayer

Leader: Jesus taught us to care for others. One way
we can care for others is by praying for them.
As we pray and sing our song, remember
the people you want to pray for.

🎵 **Caring for Others**

("Mary Had a Little Lamb")

Jesus cares for everyone,
everyone, everyone.
We can care for everyone
just as Jesus did.

When we help, we show we care,
show we care, show we care.
When we give, we show we care
just as Jesus did.

Leader: Jesus, help us
to care for others as
you did.

All: We pray to the Lord.
Amen.

Catholic Identity Retreat

Praying for Others

Part 3   I Cherish God's Word

"The Lord is near. . . . Make your requests known to God." (Philippians 4:5–6)

LISTEN to the reading from Scripture. Pay close attention to the reading.

REFLECT on what you heard. Think about:

- God is near and welcomes your prayers. Who needs your prayers today?

SHARE your thoughts and feelings with God in prayer. Speak to God as a friend.

CONTEMPLATE or sit quietly and think about God's Word in the Scripture passage from Saint Paul's Letter to the Philippians above.

Praying for Others

Part 4   I Value My Catholic Faith

We can light a candle to pray for a special need.

Light the candle below by drawing a flame over it.
Write your friend's name on the line.

_____

Promise to pray for this friend every day.

Praying for Others

Part 5   I Celebrate Catholic Identity

Outline your hand in the space below.

Now pray the five-finger prayer. Point to each finger in the drawing, and pray one prayer for someone.

Color your hand. Remember the words "Pray for others." Do that this week.

Catholic Identity Retreat

Praying for Others

Part 6 I Honor My Catholic Identity

Leader: At Mass we pray the Prayer of the Faithful. In this prayer, we pray for others. We remember the needs of all God's People. Complete the prayer with me: We pray for our Church and world leaders, especially_____. Let us pray to the Lord.

All: Lord, hear our prayer.

Leader: We pray for those who have died, especially _____. Let us pray to the Lord.

All: Lord, hear our prayer.

Leader: We pray for our community and the world, especially_____. Let us pray to the Lord.

All: Lord, hear our prayer.

Leader: God of goodness, fill our hearts. Help us to pray for all people everywhere.

All: Amen.

Catholic Identity Retreat

Bringing the Retreat Home

Praying for Others

Retreat Recap

Review the pages of your child's *Celebrating Catholic Identity: Prayer* retreat. Ask your child to tell you about the retreat. Talk about praying for others:

- Jesus taught us to care for others.
- We care for others by praying for them.
- One time that we pray for others is at Mass.

Votive Offerings

In this retreat, your child explored votive offerings by artistically "lighting" a candle. Pray about any special intentions for your family. You may wish to light candles in your parish church for these intentions.

Take a Moment

Invite your child to tell you about the people or groups of people he or she prayed for during the retreat. Together identify a way for your family to help these people beyond praying for them, and carry it out. For example, if your child prayed for homeless or poor people, you might donate your time or goods to a homeless shelter or food pantry.

Family Prayer

Pray together this prayer for people in need.

Good Shepherd,
Call us forth to speak your Word,
 To feed your sheep. . . .
For the sake of our sisters and brothers
for the sake of our world. . .
 we pray. . .
Call us forth.

(from *Call Us Forth, Catholic Relief Services*)

For more resources, see the *Catholic Identity Home Companion* at the end of this book.

Why We Believe
As a Catholic Family

What if someone asks us:

- Why does the Church pray for both the living and the dead?

The following resources can help us to respond:

The Communion of Saints is the union of all the baptized members of the Church:

- on earth—These members respond to God's grace by being baptized, living a good moral life, remaining in God's friendship, and becoming role models for one another.
- in Heaven—These members lived lives of holiness on earth and now share in the joy of eternal life with God.
- in Purgatory—These members are being prepared for Heaven, being purified from their sins.

We on earth pray for one another, both for members of the Church on earth and for those in Purgatory, that we may enter into eternal life with God just as the saints have done.

☙ What does Scripture say?

"For if he were not expecting the fallen to rise again, it would have been useless and foolish to pray for them in death." (2 Maccabees 12:44)

"[God] rescued us from such great danger of death, and he will continue to rescue us; in him we have put our hope [that] he will also rescue us again, as you help us with prayer, so that thanks may be given by many on our behalf for the gift granted us through the prayers of many." (2 Corinthians 1:10 –11)

We pray that those who have died may know God's love and mercy and may one day share in eternal life. And because the saints are closely united to Christ, they pray for us, constantly helping the Church to grow in holiness.

☙ What does the Church say?

"All who die in God's grace and friendship, but still imperfectly purified, are indeed assured of their eternal salvation; but after death they undergo purification, so as to achieve the holiness necessary to enter the joy of heaven" (CCC, 1030).

"Let us help and commemorate them. If Job's sons were purified by their father's sacrifice, why would we doubt that our offerings for the dead bring them some consolation? Let us not hesitate to help those who have died and to offer our prayers for them." (Saint John Chrysostom as quoted in CCC, 1032)

Notes:

PROJECT DISCIPLE

Pray
Learn
Celebrate
Share
Choose
Live

God's Great Gifts

Read Along

Grammy took Jason by the hand. "I have a surprise for you," she said. "Do you remember the seeds we planted?" Jason nodded his head. It seemed like that was a long, long time ago.

Jason and his grandmother walked to the garden. They went to the place where he and Grammy had dug a hole and put in the seeds. There Jason saw a bright red flower.

Jason laughed and jumped in the air. "We did it, Grammy! We grew flowers!" Grammy smiled. "We planted the seeds," she said. "God made the flowers grow. Let's tell God how happy we are."

Jason and his grandmother sat down on a bench. Grammy prayed, "We are so happy, God. You fill our world with good things." Jason thought, "God made Grammy, too." That made Jason even happier!

What makes you happy?

Because *We Believe*

God made all things.
They make us happy.

We thank God for all his gifts.

All things are gifts from God. What good things do you see around you?

 Name or draw one of your favorite things.

Talk about ways that your family can thank God for all his gifts.

Look for something in your home that makes you want to thank God.

Tell a story about why it is so special.

Pray Together

Dear God,
Thank you for

_____

_____

Amen.

PROJECT DISCIPLE

Pray
Learn
Celebrate
Share
Choose
Live

Family Fun

Look at the pictures.

What things can families do to have fun?

Because *We Believe*

Families have special ways to share God's love.

God wants families to spend time together.

God helps us to be safe.

Name people in your neighborhood who help keep us safe.

What are ways our families help keep us safe?

Talk about ways families can share God's love.

Share one place your family has fun together.

Share one place your family prays together.

Pray Together

Strong and faithful God, keep our family safe from harm. Make us a blessing to all those we meet today.

Amen.

Adapted from *Catholic Household Blessings and Prayers*

Take Home

Doing What Jesus Wants Us to Do

Pray Learn Celebrate Share Choose Live

Read Along

Katie's mother is tired. She has worked hard all day. Now it is time to fix dinner.

Katie wants to go outside to play. Her friend, Carla, has a new bike. Carla said she would let Katie ride it.

Katie thinks to herself. She then goes into the kitchen.

"Mama, can I help set the table?" Katie asks.

How did Katie help her mother?

Because *We Believe*

Jesus helped many people.

Jesus wants us to be kind and caring.

Jesus wants us to love and help one another.

Think of one way you can help someone when you are:

- at school
- on the playground
- in church
- at a store.

Write two other places you can help someone.

_____

_____

Talk about the ways Jesus wants us to love each other.

Pray Together

Make up a prayer with your family.

Ask Jesus to help you be kind and loving to one another.

The Holy Spirit Came

Jesus promised to send
the Holy Spirit.
Mary and the friends
of Jesus waited.
They prayed together.

Fold

They went out to tell all
the people about Jesus.

4

2

The Holy Spirit came.

3

Mary and the friends of Jesus were very happy.

Fold

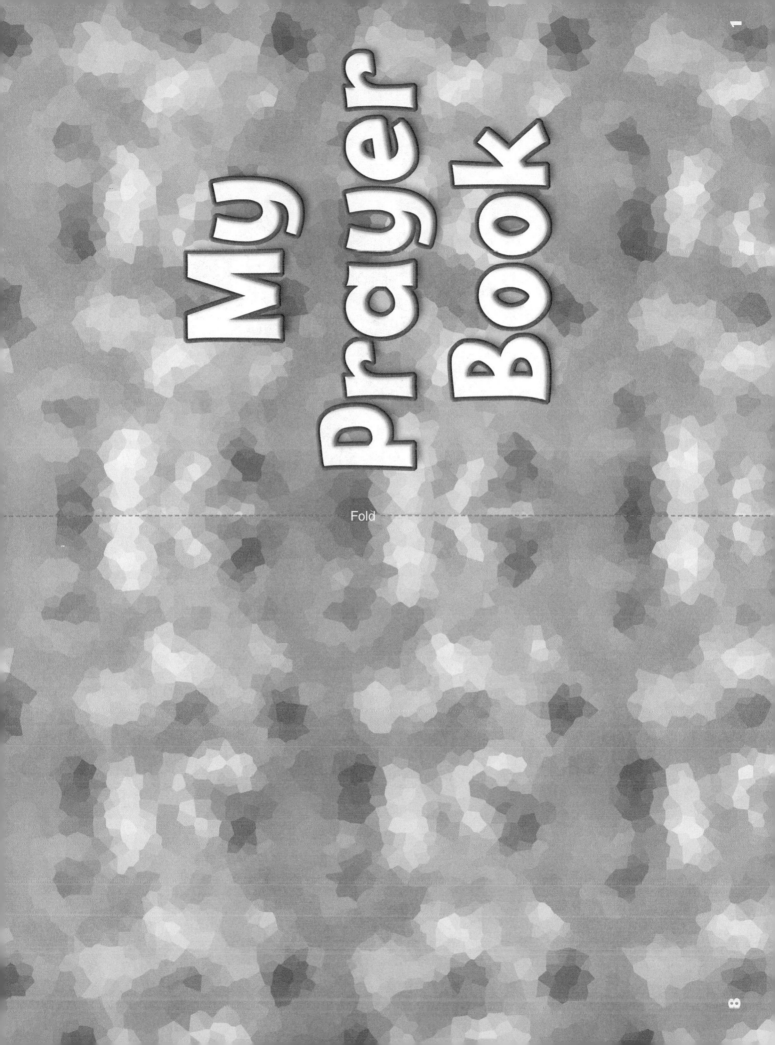

My Prayer Book

Fold

Sign of the Cross

In the name of the Father,
and of the Son,
and of the Holy Spirit.
Amen.

---- Fold ----

Grace After Meals

We give you thanks, almighty God,
for these and all your gifts
which we have received
through Christ our Lord.
Amen.

Our Father

Our Father, who art in heaven,
hallowed be thy name;
thy kingdom come;
thy will be done on earth
as it is in heaven.
Give us this day our daily bread;
and forgive us our trespasses
as we forgive those who trespass
against us;
and lead us not into temptation,
but deliver us from evil.
Amen.

Fold

Grace Before Meals

Bless us, O Lord,
and these your gifts,
which we are about to receive
from your goodness.
Through Christ our Lord.
Amen.

Hail Mary

Hail Mary, full of grace,
the Lord is with you!
Blessed are you among women,
and blessed is the fruit of
    your womb, Jesus.
Holy Mary, Mother of God,
pray for us sinners,
now and at the hour of our death.
Amen.

Fold

Glory Be to the Father

Glory be to the Father
and to the Son
and to the Holy Spirit,
as it was in the beginning
is now, and ever shall be
world without end.
Amen.

Index

The following is a list of topics that appear in the pupil's text.
Boldface indicates an entire chapter.

Congratulations!

_____

has successfully completed

the Kindergarten

We Believe

CATHOLIC IDENTITY program.

Catholic Identity

_____
Catechist/Teacher

_____
Principal/Director of Religious Education

_____
Date

End-of-Year Prayer Service

✝ **We Pray**

In the name of the Father,
and of the Son,
and of the Holy Spirit.
Amen.

Thank you, God, for our wonderful world.

Let us sing the *We Believe* song.

🎵 **We Believe, We Believe in God**

We believe in God;
We believe, we believe
    in Jesus;
We believe in the Spirit
    who gives us life.
We believe, we believe
    in God.

See you next year!

In this section, you will find questions and answers that review the content in your *We Believe: Catholic Identity Edition* book this year. Each question in this section covers the key Catholic teachings in your book, in chapter order. Answer each question to review what you have learned—whether you use this section at home, in school, or in the parish. The answers provided will strengthen your understanding of your Catholic faith and help to reinforce your Catholic Identity.

The CCC references after each answer indicate where to find further information about that answer in the *Catechism of the Catholic Church*.

Q: **What did God make?**

A: God made the whole world and everything in it. *CCC, 295*

Q: **Why did God make the whole world?**

A: God made the whole world because he loves us and cares for us. *CCC, 293*

Q: **What light did God make in the sky?**

A: God made the sun, the moon, and the stars. *CCC, 290*

CCC = Catechism of the Catholic Church

Q: **What does God want us to do with his gifts of land and water?**

A: God wants us to take care of the land and the water. *CCC, 299*

Q: **How can you thank God for the animals he made?**

A: You can thank God for the animals he made by taking care of them. *CCC, 339, 340*

Q: **How do we celebrate God's love for us?**

A: We celebrate God's love in many ways. We can celebrate by loving him, praying to him, and loving others. *CCC, 1153, 1156*

Q: **What do the celebrations in the Church year help us to remember?**

A: The celebrations in the Church year help us to remember God's love. *CCC, 1171*

Q: **What did saints always try to do?**

A: Saints always tried to share God's love with others. *CCC, 2683*

Q: Who made you?

    A: God made all people. *CCC, 355*

Q: Who is the greatest of all the saints?

    A: Mary is the greatest of all the saints. *CCC, 971*

Q: Who did God choose to be the Mother of his Son, Jesus?

    A: God chose Mary to be the Mother of his Son, Jesus. *CCC, 488*

Q: What do we celebrate at Christmas?

    A: At Christmas we celebrate the birth of the Son of God, Jesus. *CCC, 1171*

Q: Where was Jesus born?

    A: Jesus was born in a stable in Bethlehem. *CCC, 525*

Q: What is God's greatest gift to us?

    A: God's greatest gift to us is his Son, Jesus. *CCC, 458*

Q: **What is the Holy Family?**

A: The Holy Family is Jesus, Mary, and Joseph.
CCC, 1655

Q: **Where did the Holy Family live?**

A: The Holy Family lived in Nazareth. *CCC,* 533

Q: **What are some of the kind and caring things Jesus did for people?**

A: Jesus helped people who were sick. He talked to people. He listened to them. *CCC,* 1717

Q: **What did Jesus tell us about how to love others?**

A: Jesus said, "Love one another as I love you."
(John 15:12) *CCC,* 1823

Q: **How does Jesus want us to treat others?**

A: Jesus wants us to treat others with love.
CCC, 1823, 2055

Q: **Who did Jesus teach people about?**

A: Jesus, the Son of God, taught people about his Father. *CCC,* 516

Q: **What is Lent?**

A: Lent is a special time of year when we prepare for Easter. *CCC, 1438*

Q: **What is the Church?**

A: The Church is the family of God. *CCC, 759*

Q: **When do we become members of the Church?**

A: We become members of the Church at Baptism. *CCC, 1267*

Q: **What words do we pray in the Sign of the Cross?**

A: In the Sign of the Cross we pray, "In the name of the Father, and of the Son, and of the Holy Spirit. Amen." *CCC, 2157*

Q: **What is prayer?**

A: Prayer is talking to and listening to God. *CCC, 2559*

Q: **What is the prayer that Jesus taught us?**

A: Jesus taught us the Lord's Prayer. This is also called the Our Father. *CCC, 2765*

Q: What was the special meal Jesus shared with his friends, the Apostles?

A: The special meal Jesus shared with his Apostles was the Last Supper. *CCC, 610*

Q: At Mass what do the bread and wine become?

A: At Mass the bread and wine become the Body and Blood of Jesus. *CCC, 1353*

Q: Who did Jesus care about?

A: Jesus cared about everyone. *CCC, 542*

Q: When is Jesus with us?

A: Jesus is always with us. *CCC, 2743*

Q: What do we celebrate at Easter?

A: At Easter we celebrate Jesus' new life. *CCC, 1169*

Resources
for the Family

I n this section, you will find a treasury of resources to help build up your Catholic Identity at home, in your parish, and in the community. Learn more about key Catholic teachings from the themes of your child's *Celebrating Catholic Identity* retreats: **CREED**, **LITURGY & SACRAMENTS**, **MORALITY**, and **PRAYER**. For each theme, you will find Catholic prayers, practices, and devotions to share with those you love—and make a part of your daily lives as a Catholic family!

Family: "the place where parents pass on the faith to their children."

—Pope Francis
Apostolic Exhortation *Evangelii Gaudium*, 66

Spirituality and
Your Kindergartner

For your kindergartner, your home provides the basic context for faith. Kindergartners most frequently draw upon experiences of family as a way to understand God and the Church. In explaining concepts of faith to your child, you can draw upon examples of family dynamics and relationships—such as brothers and sisters, parent and child, and the understanding of family.

Your kindergartner is curious, enthusiastic, imaginative, and energetic. Your child is open to learning and is capable of understanding God's continual presence and power. Allow your child freedom to explore his or her images of God through creative art, storytelling, and play.

Kindergartners are increasing their understanding of and capacity for prayer. As a family, try to engage in various forms of prayer. Introduce your child to brief periods of silent reflection and encourage spontaneous prayers.

Kindergartners are beginning to widen their world through attendance at school and other social interactions. They are starting to move out of an egocentric stage into a more cooperative one. Encourage sharing within your family. Give your child brief opportunities to work with others as a way to further his or her capacity for cooperation.*

*See *Catechetical Formation in Chaste Living,* United States Conference of Catholic Bishops, #1

Our Loving Father

God the Father created the whole world because he loves us and he cares for us. He never leaves us and always guides us.

God gave us the Ten Commandments so that we can know how to live a life of love. The first three commandments help us to show love and respect for God. The other seven commandments help us to show love and respect for ourselves and others. Talk about ways we show respect for God and others each day.

The Ten Commandments

1. I am the LORD your God: you shall not have strange gods before me.

2. You shall not take the name of the LORD your God in vain.

3. Remember to keep holy the LORD's Day.

4. Honor your father and your mother.

5. You shall not kill.

6. You shall not commit adultery.

7. You shall not steal.

8. You shall not bear false witness against your neighbor.

9. You shall not covet your neighbor's wife.

10. You shall not covet your neighbor's goods.

All About Angels

Angels are creatures created by God as pure spirits. They do not have physical bodies. Angels serve God as his messengers. They serve God in his saving plan for us and constantly give him praise. Everyone has a guardian angel. Encourage your child to pray to his or her guardian angel.

Prayer to My Guardian Angel

Angel of God,
my guardian dear,
to whom God's love commits
 me here,
ever this day be at my side,
to light and guard,
to rule and guide.
Amen.

Book

Chapter

119   Luke, |10|

Verse

Passage Title

Titles are sometimes added to show themes of the chapters, but these titles are not part of the actual words of the Bible.

|Praise of the Father| 21 *t u**At that very moment he rejoiced [in] the holy Spirit and said, "I give you praise, Father, Lord of heaven and earth, for although you have hidden these things from the wise and the learned you have revealed them to the childlike. Yes, Father, such has been your gracious will. 22 *v*All things have been handed over to me by my Father. No one knows who the Son is except the Father, and who the Father is except the Son and anyone to whom the Son wishes to reveal him."

Passage

A passage is a section of a chapter made up of a number of verses.

This passage shows Luke 10:21–22, which means: the Gospel of Luke, chapter ten, verses twenty-one to twenty-two.

Reading the Bible . . . in Five Easy Steps

When you are given a Scripture passage to read, here are five easy steps that will help you to find it! With your child, follow these steps to look up **Lk 10:21–22**.

1. **Find the book.** When the name of the book is abbreviated, locate the meaning of the abbreviation on the contents pages at the beginning of your Bible. *Lk* stands for Luke, one of the four Gospels.

2. **Find the page.** Your Bible's contents pages will also show the page on which the book begins. Turn to that page within your Bible.

3. **Find the chapter.** Once you arrive at the page where the book begins, keep turning the pages forward until you find the right chapter. The image above shows you how a chapter number is usually displayed on a typical Bible page. You are looking for chapter **10** in Luke.

4. **Find the verses.** Once you find the right chapter, locate the verse or verses you need within the chapter. The image above also shows you how verse numbers will look on a typical Bible page. You are looking for verses **21** and **22**.

5. **Start reading!**

The Seven Sacraments

The Seven Sacraments strengthen, nourish, and heal the life of Christ in us. The sacraments change our lives. Through the sacraments the life of Christ in us continues to grow. Share with your child your experience of receiving the sacraments. If possible, show your child keepsakes or photos that help you to remember those special occasions.

The Sacraments of Christian Initiation
Baptism
Confirmation
Eucharist

The Sacraments of Healing
Penance and Reconciliation
Anointing of the Sick

The Sacraments at the Service of Communion
Holy Orders
Matrimony

The Power of Grace

How do we live as disciples of Jesus? Through the power of God's grace, we can grow in our friendship with God. Grace is a share in God's life and love. We receive grace at our Baptism and when we receive the other sacraments. Throughout our lives, grace helps us respond to God with love. It gives us the strength to live as Jesus' disciples.

Holy Days of Obligation

The liturgy is the official public prayer of the Church. In the liturgy we gather as a community joined to Christ to celebrate what we believe. The Church year is based on the life of Christ and the celebration of his life in the liturgy. The Church's year is called the liturgical year. In one liturgical year we recall and celebrate the whole life of Jesus Christ. We also honor Mary and the saints, who show us how to live as disciples of Jesus.

Each Sunday of the liturgical year is a great celebration of the Church, or a solemnity. In addition to each Sunday, there are other solemnities in the liturgical year on which we are obliged to attend Mass to give special honor to Jesus Christ for the salvation he has given to us. These are called holy days of obligation.

Holy days of obligation celebrated by the Church in the United States:

- **Solemnity of Mary, Mother of God (January 1)**
- **Ascension (when celebrated on Thursday during the Easter season*)**
- **Assumption of Mary (August 15)**
- **All Saints' Day (November 1)**
- **Immaculate Conception (December 8)**
- **Christmas (December 25)**

  Some dioceses celebrate the Ascension on the following Sunday.

Asking Forgiveness

We all need to be reconciled with God and with others. Forgiveness was an important part of Jesus' ministry. When we make mistakes, it is important to ask forgiveness. Discuss different ways to say sorry and ask for forgiveness. Say the Act of Contrition together as a family.

Act of Contrition

My God,
I am sorry for my sins with all my heart.
In choosing to do wrong
and failing to do good,
I have sinned against you
whom I should love above all things.
I firmly intend, with your help,
to do penance,
to sin no more,
and to avoid whatever leads me to sin.
Our Savior Jesus Christ
suffered and died for us.
In his name, my God, have mercy.

Peace and Justice

As disciples of Jesus, we must commit to justice and become peacemakers in every context of our lives. Justice is based on the simple fact that all people have human dignity, the value and worth that we share because God created us in his image and likeness. In Scripture, we find that God's peace, which is more than just the absence of war and violence, is realized when everyone lives in true harmony with one another and with God's creation.

"Justice will bring about peace;
    right will produce calm and security." (Isaiah 32:17)

Talk to your child about what it means to treat others justly.

Blessed Are They

What makes your family happy? When we live as Jesus' disciples, we can find true happiness. The Beatitudes are Jesus' teachings that describe the way to live as his disciples. In the Beatitudes the word *blessed* means "happy."

The Beatitudes	What the Beatitudes Mean for Us
"Blessed are the poor in spirit, for theirs is the kingdom of heaven."	We are "poor in spirit" when we depend on God and make God more important than anyone or anything else in our lives.
"Blessed are they who mourn, for they will be comforted."	We "mourn" when we are sad because of the selfish ways people treat each other.
"Blessed are the meek, for they will inherit the land."	We are "meek" when we are patient, kind, and respectful to all people, even those who do not respect us.
"Blessed are they who hunger and thirst for righteousness, for they will be satisfied."	We "hunger and thirst for righteousness" when we search for justice and treat everyone fairly.
"Blessed are the merciful, for they will be shown mercy."	We are "merciful" when we forgive others and do not take revenge on those who hurt us.
"Blessed are the clean of heart, for they will see God."	We are "clean of heart" when we are faithful to God's teachings and try to see God in all people and all situations.
"Blessed are the peacemakers, for they will be called children of God."	We are "peacemakers" when we treat others with love and respect and when we help others to stop fighting and make peace.
"Blessed are they who are persecuted for the sake of righteousness, for theirs is the kingdom of heaven." Matthew 5:3–10	We are "persecuted for the sake of righteousness" when others disrespect us for living as disciples of Jesus and following his example.

Praying the Rosary

The Rosary is among traditional expressions of prayer we call devotions. The Mysteries of the Rosary are taken from the lives of Jesus and Mary. Reflecting on each Mystery as we pray the Rosary helps to draw us in to the mystery of Jesus Christ among us.

Mysteries of the Rosary

Joyful Mysteries

The Annunciation

The Visitation

The Birth of Jesus

The Presentation of Jesus in the Temple

The Finding of the Child Jesus in the Temple

Sorrowful Mysteries

The Agony in the Garden

The Scourging at the Pillar

The Crowning with Thorns

The Carrying of the Cross

The Crucifixion and Death of Jesus

Glorious Mysteries

The Resurrection

The Ascension

The Descent of the Holy Spirit upon the Apostles

The Assumption of Mary into Heaven

The Coronation of Mary as Queen of Heaven

The Mysteries of Light

Jesus' Baptism in the Jordan

The Miracle at the Wedding at Cana

Jesus Announces the Kingdom of God

The Transfiguration

The Institution of the Eucharist

The Marriage at Cana, by Julius Schnorr von Carolsfeld (1819)

The Rosary

Praying the Rosary creates a peaceful rhythm of prayer during which we can reflect on the Mysteries of the Rosary, special times in the lives of Jesus and Mary. Follow the numbered steps to pray the Rosary.

5 Pray a Glory Be to the Father after each set of small beads.

End

6 Pray the Hail, Holy Queen to end the Rosary.

4 Pray a Hail Mary at every small bead.

3 Pray an Our Father at every large bead.

2 Then pray the Apostles' Creed.

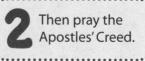

1 Start with the Sign of the Cross.

Start